P9-BEE-777

SELF HYPNOSIS AS YOU READ

42 LIFE CHANGING SCRIPTS

FORBES ROBBINS BLAIR

www.forbesrobbinsblair.com

Cover design and layout by Rob Morrison
Published in Maryland USA

Copyright © 2013 Forbes Robbins Blair.

All rights reserved. No part of this book may be reproduced in any form or by any electronic or mechanical means including information storage and retrieval systems—except in the case of brief quotations embodies in critical articles or reviews—without permission in writing from its author,
Forbes Robbins Blair.

This publication is designed to provide accurate and authoritative information in regard to the subject matter covered. It is sold with the understanding that the publisher is not engaged in rendering legal, accounting, psychological or other professional service. If expert assistance is required, the services of a competent professional person should be sought.

—From a Declaration of Principles Jointly Adopted by a Committee of the American Bar Association and a Committee of Publishers and Associations

Manufactured in the USA

Self Hypnosis As You Read / Forbes Robbins Blair.
—1st edition.

PREFACE

*"The diet starts this Monday and I'll stick
to it now. I promise!"*

*"That does it! I'm cutting up the credit
cards once and for all and I'm not wasting
any more money on things I don't need."*

*"Smoking is ruining my health. This will
absolutely be my last."*

How many times have you said one of those things?

Maybe you have a bad habit that is causing you pain,
hurting your loved ones, ruining your health, costing you
money, damaging your career or just wasting your time.
Fortunately, there is a fast and effective way to remove those
unwanted habits: *Self Hypnosis as You Read: 42 Life
Changing Scripts.*

Think for a moment. What are your bad habits costing
you in money, business, health, relationships? You know the
habits I'm talking about: not taking care of your body, neglect-
ing relationships, working too hard, stress eating,
mismanaging your money.

Bad habits chip away at the life you could be living now.
They prevent you from enjoying fulfilling relationships. They
halt your potential. They keep you from looking and feeling
your best.

Habits are patterns of thinking and acting that become
ingrained because they are frequently repeated over a span of
time. Here's an example. Let's say you realize that stress is
making your blood pressure go through the roof, hurting your
health. So you make a promise to manage your stress better.
However, your efforts don't last and you become even more

stressed as your blood pressure remains high. Willpower alone did not work. You need something more.

To illustrate how willpower alone is not enough, let me tell you a story. A teacher wants to help her sixth-grade class understand the power of habits. She takes a bit of light thread and wraps it one time around a student's wrist. And she tells the student: "This string represents the power of doing something one time. Can you break it?"

He easily breaks the string.

The teacher then wraps the string around the student's wrist several times and repeats the challenge to break it. The student finds it too strong to break. And the teacher tells the class, "That's the power of repeated actions."

The lesson? Changing repeated patterns takes more than personal strength. It requires a different approach.

Within this book are 42 self hypnosis scripts for various topics from saving money to overcoming health problems. When you use the scripts along with the proven self hypnosis as-you-read method, you will break those habits and be transformed.

Imagine how it will feel to let go of what is holding you back. Think of the confidence you will have as your body, your attitude and your abilities are changed forever. Your friends, family and colleagues will be amazed. They will marvel how you were able to achieve so much so fast.

Recently I received a remarkable email from a mother whose teenaged son was having severe troubles in school. He was once a happy, good student and a gifted soccer player who became withdrawn, lonely, depressed and—"broken and defeated."

She was understandably distraught about this. After having tried therapists, prayer and affirmations—nothing worked. As a last ditch effort, she had him work with my as-you-read self hypnosis technique.

She was excited to tell me that after he used it for only five sessions everything changed for him: "He got straight A's, stood up to a bully and made an elite soccer team!" She was extremely grateful and called it a "miracle."

I love getting letters like hers! Her son is an inspiration to me because he was determined to lift himself up from that situation. All he needed was the right tool.

So many times, I have heard people say they want positive change only to give up before they give it more than a minimal effort.

If any of that describes you, here are the questions I would ask before you start to change your habits: Do you have a plan? Are you willing to stick with it? Are you positive enough? Are you committed?

Going forward, I would suggest you get rid of self-talk like "I would've," or "I should've," or "I could've." Leave the excuses behind. Dream big. Be positive. Make it happen.

Allow this book to help you. Commit to daily sessions until you reach each goal. It's easy. And you *will* get there.

Enjoy your new life,

Forbes Robbins Blair

Happiness depends upon ourselves.

ARISTOTLE

CONTENTS

INTRODUCTION

Words are powerful. They carry the potential to inspire, to encourage, to promote healing. Or, they can cause hurt and damage us for life.

Remember the playgrounds of childhood and the cutting words the kids might say: "Fatty, skinny, ugly, stupid!"?

After that, perhaps your mother tried to comfort you by saying, "Sticks and stones may break your bones but words will never hurt you." But something was missing because the kids' words continued to hurt.

Positive words are powerful too. Remember how you felt to have someone praise your creativity or your determination? Or when they said, "Hey, you look really good today"? To this day, their positive words are sources of encouragement and improve your self confidence.

However, it is the words *we* say about and to *ourselves* that are most powerful. They are like mental scripts we recite that dictate, often to a large degree, our quality of life. They shape how we feel, what we believe, what we are willing to do, and the limit we put on our potential.

These inner scripts can make all the difference whether we succeed or fail to enjoy happy and fulfilling lives.

When we hear the word "scripts" we think of plays, movies or television shows which actors memorize and recite. The self hypnosis scripts in this book are to be read out loud as well, only you will not need to memorize anything. You will simply read them while you follow some easy instructions. The self hypnosis as-you-read method does the rest.

Self Hypnosis as You Read: 42 Life Changing Scripts is about positively altering your inner dialogue and changing the negative scripts that circulate in your head.

Are You New to this Method?

If you are unfamiliar with my hypnosis as-you-read technique, let me catch you up.

My name is Forbes Robbins Blair and I am a clinical hypnosis therapist who sees clients mostly for behavior challenges like smoking cessation, weight loss and confidence building. Since 1997, I have been passionate about my work and I see it as a helping profession.

Within the first two years of my professional practice, I made an amazing discovery—that a person can be hypnotized while they read hypnotic scripts designed for that purpose. Virtually any literate person who can concentrate in an average way can use this technique to change their lives in practical ways.

In 2004, I released what became a bestselling book on the subject, *Instant Self Hypnosis: How to Hypnotize Yourself with Your Eyes Open.* In 2011, I published a popular sequel called *More Instant Self Hypnosis: Hypnotize Yourself as You Read.* People from all over the world have contacted me to share their triumphs with the technique and the scripts in those books. I am happy to say that the method and scripts have a long track record of success.

The method only takes about 20 minutes a day for a few days. You first read an induction script that puts you in a hypnotic state. A suggestion script for your goal follows. To finish, you read a Wake Up segment that safely brings you back to everyday consciousness. You repeat that session once a day for a few days and watch as your life automatically transforms!

Real Success, Real People

Here is a true story that may help you understand why I have such confidence in self hypnosis as-you-read:

2

Myra is an inspirational woman who requested a custom-written hypnosis script from me to help control the panic attacks she had while undergoing MRI scans.

It was a problem that started when she was a child. One day while she was playing, Myra explored a hope chest when suddenly the top fell down and locked her inside. Terrified, she was forced to experience that scary darkness for hours until her friends got to her house and opened the chest to set her free.

That incident began a lifelong fear of enclosed spaces. So when she attempted to get her first MRI scan, she felt so panicked she could not finish it.

She told me she read my first book, *Instant Self Hypnosis*, and loved the results she experienced with other issues. She also said its hypnosis method was superior to others she had tried. So she was determined to use it to face her "MRI problem" by using the as-you-read self hypnosis method.

She asked me to write a custom script to help her control the panic she felt during the MRI scan. So I researched the subject and came up with the best script I could write just for her. I finished it and sent it to her asking her to let me know the MRI scan turned out.

A couple of weeks later, she emailed about how she felt:

Mr. Forbes,

Just wanted to let you know that I had a successful MRI Scan! :)

The doctor on duty decided to give me a very tiny dose of something to decrease my heart rate, but it was my using the self-hypnosis script 2x a day from when first received that truly helped. I knew it was going to go well when I slept like a baby the night before without any medication! I even did one last self-hypnosis session that morning.

Once they laid me down on the MRI bed, I began to envision myself on that little small wooden boat with a gentle breeze caressing me, kept doing the instructed breathing technique while thinking: "Calm and Comfortable"; I even found myself choreographing a workout routine to the rhythm of sounds that were coming from the MRI Machine for next day's 5:45 AM Bootcamp Class that I lead.

When I realized that I was doing that, I had to fight off a fit of giggles that threatened to overtake me which caused the Nurse to chide me to stay still. The Self-hypnosis script you sent me had stated that I might even find the MRI Scan process amusing, and I did! :)

Thanks again for everything. I am using your Instant Self-Hypnosis to reach other goals, and am looking forward to my continued success!

Gratefully yours,

Myra I. Colmenero-Macmillan

It's because of people like Myra that I continue to find passion and excitement for this amazing self-hypnosis technique! This method and its scripts have worked wonders for many people. They will also work for you!

More Challenges, More Scripts

Self Hypnosis As You Read: 42 Life Changing Scripts is my fourth book. It features a collection of therapeutic self hypnosis scripts based on topics requested from the readers of my other books. Some scripts target self-improvement goals. Other scripts handle health and addiction challenges.

In my work, I have even seen serious medical issues improve or go into remission because of hypnosis. Therefore, because readers have requested them I decided to include scripts for several challenges like "Fibromyalgia Relief" and "Shrink Cancerous Tumors."

However, those scripts are not a replacement for medical, psychological or professional advice. Let your medical professional know if you plan to use the scripts from this book. The chances are good your doctor will approve.

Also featured in this book are scripts that center on very personal issues such as addictions to pornography and masturbation. Challenges like these are often embarrassing for people to share with a therapist, so this book offers a private way to overcome them.

Of all of the 42 scripts in this book, the one I recommend the most is "Perpetual Stress Relief." I believe that many challenges are caused or made worse by the constant stress that taxes the human body's nervous system. The primary source of that stress is often the pressures of modern life. Whatever the cause, regular use of the Perpetual Stress Relief script will not only help to alleviate that stress, but it may relieve some other issues at the same time!

I have also included several hypnotic inductions. Each induction script takes a slightly different approach to help different personality types. Try each induction and see which one works best for your needs.

How to Use This Book

This book is easy to use. You can begin very soon. First, let me describe each section:

- The first chapter is called BASICS. It introduces the disciplines of hypnosis and self hypnosis. It also briefly introduces you to the as-you-read method. (If you are new to the method, please read it fully.)

- The METHOD chapter gives you specific instructions about how the technique works and how to get the best results. Then, you are encouraged to use an induction script called "Master Induction 3.0." You will analyze your experience so you are comfortable and confident with the technique.

- The chapter called INDUCTIONS features four separate induction scripts that hypnotize you as you read them. My previous self hypnosis books focused on only one induction. Here, you will select one of the four inductions to read before you combine it with the goal script of your choice in the next chapter.

- The chapter SCRIPTS contains self hypnosis as-you-read scripts for a wide range of self-improvement and therapeutic topics. You will select a script to read after you have hypnotized yourself with one of the inductions from the previous chapter. At the end of each script is a short narrative called The Wake Up which guides you back safely to your usual state of mind.

- The chapter called QUESTIONS provides answers to the most common questions about the method and the scripts.

- The last chapter, called ADVANCED, contains four advanced techniques to take your efforts to the next level.

- The book wraps up with a brief SUPPORT message; information about me as the AUTHOR; and RESOURCES which might interest you.

If you are ready to change your life, let's get started!

BASICS

In this chapter I discuss the basics about hypnosis and self hypnosis. Then I explain how I discovered the self hypnosis as-you-read method.

If you are new to hypnosis and self hypnosis, this BASICS chapter is essential reading. However, if you have read *Instant Self Hypnosis: How to Hypnotize Yourself with Your Eyes Open* or its sequel *More Instant Self Hypnosis: Hypnotize Yourself as You Read* you may move on to the chapter called INDUCTIONS.

What Happens When You Are Hypnotized

Did you know that there is no agreement for the precise definition of hypnosis? In one of my previous books, I wrote that hypnosis is a condition of relaxation and heightened suggestibility. Generally, that definition works very well. It's certainly part of the picture. However, there is much more to hypnosis.

Hypnosis allows a part of your conscious, critical mind to relax—the part with all those doubts and fears that often stand in the way of your progress. While hypnotized, your mind can embrace new ideas, attitudes and behaviors so you can overcome longstanding negative patterns.

That is the reason it is successfully used so often as a therapeutic tool. So, for example, when you are hypnotized it becomes easy to accept that you feel confident or more outgoing. You can perform complex tasks more easily.

> When you are hypnotized you easily
> absorb suggestions to think, feel and
> do things you usually find difficult.

You are not asleep when you are hypnotized. You do not turn into someone's puppet. You remain aware and awake. You refrain from doing anything contrary to your moral code. You easily reject any questionable hypnotic suggestions. You are in control at all times.

Hypnosis is not weird or supernatural. It is a natural and fun phenomenon that can be used to communicate with your inner mind to allow positive changes in thought and behavior.

Hypnosis in Everyday Life

I am amused when people say they can't be hypnotized because most people are naturally hypnotized in one form or another every day of their lives. They just don't realize it. Think about it, and you will agree that we regularly subject ourselves to influences that bypass our critical thinking.

Many experts consider the "critical bypass of the mind" to be an accurate definition of hypnosis. Let me explain further. Whenever you sit in front of the television and laugh at an enjoyable scripted show, you are allowing yourself to be hypnotized. You willingly suspend your disbelief. You permit yourself to believe in the reality of the people and situations on the screen. The critic of the mind—the part that knows that this is fictional—is bypassed, which allows you to immerse yourself in that experience.

During the show, you experience a genuine rush of excitement during an action sequence or a peal of laughter because of a sitcom joke or a tearfulness when a favorite character dies—all of these emotions are involuntary physical responses to something imaginary!

That may sound like no big deal until you realize how hard it is to make yourself authentically cry or laugh on command without calling upon your imagination or memory to do so. If you don't believe me, go ahead and try it now: laugh! And not a fake or forced one, but the kind of laugh that is honestly based on passion or emotion.

See what I mean? One of the amazing aspects of hypnosis is that you can access authentic emotions and trigger physiological responses with nothing more than the power of suggestion and imagination.

Everyday hypnosis also comes to us in the form of recurring suggestions from commercial advertisements. Adver-tisers know that if they repeatedly expose people to their products a large number of them will eventually buy. Repetition of an idea or suggestion is a remarkably effective way to bypass the mind's critical faculty. Such repetition is a common hypnotic technique.

You will also find hypnosis at work in your local church or temple, in the military, at school, the doctor's office, and even in the workplace. These institutions use a wide array of covert verbal and non-verbal devices to direct the thinking and behavior in their audiences. Wherever there are uniforms, music, pageantry, philosophies, dogma, peer pressure and charismatic authority figures, hypnosis is at work.

Virtually *everyone* has been hypnotized in various ways—even within the last 24 hours. So the person who believes he cannot be hypnotized is usually mistaken. As long you can concentrate for even a short time, you are hypnotizable.

How Hypnosis Works

Therapeutic hypnosis *openly* uses a set of techniques to accomplish life changes.

There are many methods a hypnotist may use to hypnotize someone. However, no matter what method is used a person must want to be hypnotized or little will happen. Compliance is absolutely essential. There must be no fear or distrust of the hypnotic process or failure will likely result. Fear and non-compliance act as barriers to effective hypnosis, and even the best hypnotist in the world will find them difficult to overcome.

Also, there must also be a positive expectation of success for the individual being hypnotized. When the person expects and imagines they are going to be hypnotized, their mind helps to fulfill that expectation. If she or he perceives the hypnotist to be knowledgeable, capable and trustworthy, and they clearly understands what to expect from hypnosis, success will follow.

> Imagination and expectation play such large roles
> in the hypnotic process, they can be used to
> hypnotize without assistance from
> any other technique.

I have had many clients come to me in person after reading my books. And I am glad they feel like they know me and can trust me. They believe I am an expert. They follow my instructions without reservation and effortlessly enter hypnosis with the simplest of inductions. You might say they have been pre-conditioned to be successfully hypnotized by me.

That certainly makes my role easy. In some cases, I have merely told pre-conditioned clients to close their eyes and relax deeper as I counted backwards from ten to one. By the time I had reached the number five they were already in a deep, receptive state of hypnosis!

Because they accepted what I said to be true, because they had no fear of the process, and because they followed my instructions—they fulfilled their own expectations.

Again, I communicated with them to establish trust. I discussed their level of comfort and their expectations. They slipped easily into a condition of heightened suggestibility. After that, I delivered a few minutes of post-hypnotic suggestions that targeted their goal. I finished by emerging them from hypnosis.

The point is this: your mindset is the most important factor for whether you will be successful with hypnosis. So it's in your best interest to approach your sessions with confidence you will succeed. You need to let go of all fears. Do not be defiant. Recognize its easy simplicity. Absorb the strength of the outcome and you will get superb results.

There are many ways you can be formally hypnotized. Many hypnotists use carefully worded narrations that get you to relax and get into a narrowed state of attention.

Under hypnosis, your mind can easily accept ideas for positive change. For example, when hypnotized you are able to absorb the suggestion that "You are now and shall evermore remain a non-smoker." Without hypnosis, that suggestion would most likely be rejected by the conscious mind because of the belief that it is hard to stop smoking. However, when hypnotized, the critical voice of the mind is subdued and the new idea is accepted by the subconscious part of your mind where habits are formed. Whatever the subconscious mind accepts as true affects the physical body. If your mind accepts the suggestion that "your body rejects smoking and finds the smell of cigarettes repugnant," your body's responses to cigarettes will change! It is because of the mind/body connection that hypnosis is such a powerful and versatile tool.

After the hypnotist has issued suggestions for the intended goal, the person is emerged from the hypnotic condition. This is often done by instructing the person to return to the everyday state of mind.

What Happens After You Are Hypnotized

After you are hypnotized, you may be completely unaware you were hypnotized at all! This is common because some people expect hypnosis to feel weird or to cause amnesia. It usually doesn't. More often, being hypnotized feels natural and relaxing.

In fact, a wise hypnotherapist will point out how successful the session was.

If a person doubts they were hypnotized, the post-hypnotic suggestions imparted will likely not be effective. And thoughts like, *"I wasn't really hypnotized. This didn't work for me."* can override an otherwise effective hypnosis session and negate all therapeutic success.

Do It Yourself with Self Hypnosis

Self hypnosis refers to hypnosis you perform on yourself to achieve success without the need for an external hypnotist.

To the uniformed, the idea of self hypnosis can be puzzling because they do not understand how it works. For instance, I ran into a woman in a local bookstore who laughed at the idea of self hypnosis books as she said: *"How would a self hypnotized person ever wake up!?"*

She was under the false, common impression that a person is unconscious while hypnotized. The opposite is true: during both hypnosis and self hypnosis a person is aware and awake at all times, only more relaxed and receptive. To "wake up" from self hypnosis is a matter of using willpower or intention to return to your everyday state of mind.

There are many ways to self hypnotize. Perhaps the simplest way is to get into a very relaxed condition while you remain awake. This may be accomplished through the application of one or more techniques. You could relax parts of your body one at a time. You could use relaxing imagery. You could count your breaths or some other counting procedure to progressively relax your body and the mind. Once they are calmed and relaxed, suggestions for change or improvement are delivered. Then it's time to emerge or wake up from self hypnosis. To assist that, a counting procedure is frequently used.

. One common way to make the self hypnosis process easier is to record a hypnotic script and listen to it as you close your eyes and follow instructions. This has the advantage of guiding you into hypnosis without the common snare of losing track of the session.

Still, the possibility of falling asleep with an hypnosis audio remains.

Often a self hypnosis session requires repetition to achieve full results. There are no hard rules about how often to repeat a session because everyone responds differently. I recommend you repeat a session once or twice a day until you achieve the change you want.

More Advantages

The advantages of self hypnosis are many.

Cost is one advantage. If you can hypnotize yourself effectively, there is no need to leave your home to visit a costly hypnotherapist.

You can do self hypnosis virtually any time or anywhere. Just find a few comfortable, private minutes. The sessions can be as short as five minutes or go all the way to an hour, although the sessions in this book take just 20 minutes.

Not only is self hypnosis a great way to work on your troubles, it is as relaxing and soothing as a meditation session or an afternoon nap. Those calming effects alone are worthwhile because many irritating or debilitating challenges have their source in accumulated stress. In fact, self hypnosis is an easy way to relieve that stress while you work on your other areas of self-improvement.

How I Discovered Self Hypnosis as You Read

A marvelous feature of the self hypnosis as-you-read technique is you do not need to record the scripts or memorize anything. Instead, you can hypnotize yourself with your eyes open while you read a script aloud.

The concept is based on a discovery I made shortly after I became certified to do clinical hypnotherapy. One day, while I was rehearsing a script for a custom hypnosis audio spoken out loud, I entered into a state of hypnosis. I knew I was hypnotized because I had been trained to recognize those signs. After reading just a few paragraphs of the script, I felt unusually relaxed and spaced out—as if everything was a projection or a dream. And when the phone rang loudly, I became suddenly extremely agitated. Those experiences indicated significant levels of hypnosis.

While reading the script aloud I had hypnotized myself with my eyes-open! After that phenomenal experience, I searched all of my hypnosis books and the internet for discussions about it but there was nothing.

I had discovered something unique—
a self hypnosis method other
hypnotists were not talking about.

I began composing hypnotic scripts designed to be read aloud to tackle some of my own self-improvement challenges. I wrote one script to help me to lose ten pounds; I wrote another to enjoy myself better at parties; and another to overcome serious procrastination. Then I read each script once a day for several consecutive days, then less often over a period of weeks. To my utter delight, I reached all three goals!

Not only had the method worked, it actually performed *better* than traditional eyes closed self hypnosis and audio recordings I used. And I did not run into the difficulty of having to memorize post-hypnotic suggestions. I did not fall asleep either.

This was the most effective form of
self hypnosis I had ever experienced!

What I really appreciated is the way the script-reading method guarantees more involvement. With other forms of self hypnosis, or even with 1-on-1 hypnosis, serious lapses of attention are commonplace and problematic. On the other hand, with self hypnosis as-you-read, you must pay attention.

I knew I had discovered something remarkable. So I decided to develop it and then test it some more. I began to teach the method at a local adult learning center. Students were intrigued and excited and reported excellent results.

I wanted to share my discovery with a larger audience. So in 2004, *Instant Self Hypnosis: How to Hypnotize Yourself with Your Eyes Open* was published, which I'm pleased to say, remains very well-received by self hypnosis and self-help enthusiasts all over the world. Even university psychology professors have recommended it to their students.

After the release of *Instant Self Hypnosis*, I refined the technique and found ways to make the scripts even better. But "better" does not mean it's more complicated. One of the reasons many people love this method is because it is so easy to use. I've decided to keep it that way.

You can try it yourself in the next chapter.

METHOD

This chapter explains how self hypnosis as-you-read works. You will then be guided to experience it for yourself and to analyze your experience with it.

How It Works

The method is straightforward: You first read aloud an induction script designed to hypnotize you. Once you have read it, you will be in a state of as-you-read self hypnosis and highly receptive to beneficial suggestions.

You then read aloud a goal script with post-hypnotic suggestions that target your goal. This script is a series of carefully worded sentences composed to have a strong impact on your subconscious—the part of you that makes positive change happen.

To finish the session, you read aloud The Wake Up section, which brings you back to everyday consciousness easily and gently. That concludes your session.

When you finish reading, you go about your day and your behavior changes in subtle or obvious ways.

Sometimes results show up after just one reading of the script. More often, it takes several repetitions to get the full benefit. I recommend you perform the sessions once a day for three and twelve consecutive days. Most people find benefits fully manifest around the seventh day. Results vary depending on the person and the nature of the issue.

The beauty of the method is that all of the hard work has been done for you by these scripts. Your job is to select the induction and the suggestion script for your goal and read them once a day until you succeed.

If you commit to the method, you can look forward to remarkable changes in your life.

Why It Works

There are several mechanisms at work that help produce a hypnotic state:

- *When you read aloud, hearing your voice can even induce hypnosis.* By speaking in your own calm and quieting vocal tones, you become your own hypnotist—relaxing both your nervous system and mind.

- *The words and phrases are hypnotically-engineered.* The inductions contain language and imagery composed specifically to have a hypnotic effect on whoever reads them.

- *The conscious mind and its natural critic are kept busy by scanning the lines of text.* This distraction—when combined with the hypnotic text and your calming vocalizations—is very useful because it bypasses the self-sabotaging effect the rational mind can have when attempting to change a longstanding habit.

- *The combination of reading and hearing the words enhances their hypnotic impact.* Some people absorb suggestions better when they hear them, others when they see and/or read them. This method uses both forms of input, visual and auditory, which contributes to success.

- *Safety and control are maintained at all times.* Since it is clear that you must remain aware and awake at all times to read the words, any irrational fear of losing control during hypnosis is eliminated. And when you feel safe and relaxed about your sessions, it becomes easier to hypnotize yourself.

- *Completed hypnosis sessions every time.* Because the words are scripted, you are assured you will read and absorb all of the targeted suggestions every time you put the technique to work.

Your First Session

Your first session using the self hypnosis as-you-read method introduces you to the method. After all, experience is the best teacher. This first session does not target a personal self-improvement goal. This is a hypnotic primer to boost later sessions when you use any of the scripts in this book.

During this session, you are going to read the *Master Induction 3.0* and The Wake Up at the end. The whole session will take you about 20 minutes.

Not only will you get introduced to an actual self hypnosis as-you-read session, but you will also absorb post-hypnotic suggestions so that you respond quickly and easily to any of the 42 scripts in this book. If you are new to the self hypnosis as-you-read method it is an important place to start so give it your full effort. Carefully read and follow the instructions provided.

Preparation and Reading Instructions

- Find a quiet comfortable place to read where you will not be disturbed for 20 minutes.

- Sit in a comfortable chair or sofa where you can relax as you read the script.

- Read the script *aloud*. While people have reported success when reading silently (such as my deaf readers), reading aloud is the preferred method to achieve maximum effect.

- As you read use a relaxed and gentle tone of voice, like you would read to calm a young child.

- Read the induction part of the session *s-l-o-w-l-y*.

- You do not need to read the word in parentheses out loud. However, follow the instructions they contain.

- When directed to pause and imagine something, take the time to do so. It will pay off!

- Pause for a couple of seconds wherever you see three dots (...)

- Pause three to five seconds between each paragraph.

- Emphasize any italicized words.

- Read the entire script in one session, including The Wake Up. Even though you could naturally emerge from self hypnosis on your own, it provides a quick and efficient way to safely return to your everyday state of mind.

Master Induction 3.0

(to be read aloud)

"I hypnotize myself as I read. Right now ... I find myself in a quiet and comfortable space where I can *easily concentrate* on these words as I gently read them aloud.

"With the sound of my voice I *soothe my nervous system* ... calm my entire body and relax my thoughts. I speak slowly ... with a gentle but resonant tone, as if I was reading a bedtime story to a young child who is getting ready to ... go to sleep. The slower I read the more relaxed the child becomes.

"I make believe everything moves in *slow motion* ... (read slower) ... slow motion ... (read even slower) ... slow motion. And moment by moment, my mind clears like the surface of a quiet mountain lake. Clear ... calm ... quiet.

"I picture myself relaxing in a small and sturdy boat that drifts gently on a glassy lake. The lake is surrounded by tall, majestic trees. The sun shines and warms my skin.

"The golden rays on my face ... relax my cheeks and loosen my jaw ... and as they do, my thoughts and feelings relax and loosen too ... so that these *words and ideas flow* from my lips ... and flow effortlessly into my mind ... relaxing me twice as deeply.

"I feel the healing golden sunshine on my neck and shoulders ... and it goes down my arms ... into my hands ... the gentle heat caresses each of my fingers and fingertips ... so much so that my fingers may feel different. They may feel warmer ... or tingle a bit ... or maybe my fingers just feel much more relaxed than before.

"And I can imagine these waves of *relaxing warmth* spread throughout my chest ... cascade down my solar plexus ... pass through the pelvic region ... and go through my legs ... warm comfortable light ... extending into my feet and toes. It is a wonderful sensation.

"It feels so good that I imagine I close my eyes as I drift on the safe vessel. I listen to the leaves of the trees rustling ... (pause a moment and imagine you hear the rustling) ... and I feel a refreshing breeze pass over my body ... (take a few seconds to see this) ... and I enjoy the sweet fragrance of wildflowers on the wind ... (imagine the scent of flowers).

"I am filled with an incredible sense of peace and well-being as I just allow my mind and the boat to move and drift ... carefree ... along the mirror-like surface of the serene water. Just drifting now ... into gentle pathways of peace and solace ... easily ... effortlessly ... the way I might feel on the border of a sound ... deep ... sleep ... (read very slowly) ... a sound ... deep ... *sleep.*

"When I open my eyes I discover the boat has come to a stop upon a lush island where abundant green plant life looks well cared for. I notice a trail that leads to a magnificent mansion. As I step out of the boat and slowly walk the trail toward the mansion, I *feel mesmerized* by the amazing architecture and magnificence of the great manor.

"I come to a closed iron gate where a formidable guard stands looking at me with a hard glare. But that glare quickly turns to a grin because the guard recognizes me and opens the gate saying, 'Welcome home.' I now realize the mansion belongs to me and that the guard knows me and works for me.

"I walk through the gate and up to a splendid, ornate door where my own first name is embossed in pure gold. As I speak my name aloud ... (say your first name aloud) ... the door opens all by itself, as if by *some mysterious power.* As I step through the door's threshold I feel a deep sense of safety and well-being.

"There are many hallways and rooms to this mansion representing the many aspects of my mind and my life. I make my way to a short staircase with five stairs that lead down to my favorite thinking place. As I go down the stairs, I count backwards from five to one. As I do, I use my imagination to *relax even deeper* and to glide into a condition of self-hypnosis ... a state of deep relaxation and heightened receptivity ... with my eyes open.

"Five ... I imagine walking down the stairs and that I feel twice as relaxed with each number.

"Four ... the deeper I go, the more open to positive change I now become.

"Three ... effortlessly going deeper down the stairs ... feeling safe and secure yet open and receptive.

"Two ... down into a calm and comfortable place ... where creating positive changes is effortless and uncomplicated.

"One ... at the bottom of the stairs now, and I imagine what it might feel like to now be in a state of self hypnosis with my eyes open.

"I enter into a familiar, welcoming reading room. I approach the most comfortable looking chair and sit down to *relax fully*. And as I feel peaceful and supported, I pick up a small book on a table next to the chair. I read the cover with the title 'Hypnotize Yourself as You Read.' I open the book and begin to read. The words *speak to me directly* and seem to rise off the pages and into my mind. Here is what they say:

"'You are now successfully hypnotized. You are highly receptive to positive ideas and suggestions while you remain hypnotized. Every time you read any induction in this book, you automatically go deeper into hypnosis than the time before.

"You *remain deeply hypnotized* while you read suggestions corresponding to your purpose and goals. Your mind absorbs and retains desirable suggestions the way a sponge soaks in water. You easily *stay hypnotized* with your eyes open until you finish reading The Wake-Up.

"When you emerge from hypnosis you will feel refreshed and happy and you will *feel empowered* to overcome your challenges and reach your goals. You will feel a growing sense of relaxed self-assurance and optimism."

(The Wake-Up)

"I will emerge gently and easily from hypnosis now by counting from one to five. With each number I emerge twenty percent. When I reach the number five, I will return to everyday awareness.

"One ... emerging twenty percent, beginning to awaken from hypnosis now ... (speak a little louder and stronger).

"Two ... forty percent now as I become fully aware of my body and environment ... (speak louder and stronger).

"Three ... sixty percent ... I look forward to the positive results from this hypnosis session ... (speak louder and stronger).

"Four ... eighty percent, emerging peaceful and happy ... (strongly assert your intention to emerge).

"FIVE ... FIVE ... FIVE ... One hundred percent now! Wide awake and fully alert!!!"

After Your First Session

How did you like the Master Induction 3.0?

If this was your first time using the self hypnosis as-you-read method, then you probably had one of three experiences:

1. You felt hypnotized as you read during the session and now you marvel at the technique—and you believe the author is a genius.

2. You felt relaxed but are not sure whether you were hypnotized. You feel good after the session now and are noticeably eager to discover more of what the method has to offer.

3. You did not feel hypnotized. You felt nothing unusual. You wonder if this is nonsense.

If category #1 applies to you: congratulations! You are highly suggestible and can expect truly amazing things from the scripts in this book! You are one of those individuals who goes quickly and deeply into hypnosis—even the very first time you attempt it. If that describes you, keep up the good work. Since your ability is naturally strong you will not need to work hard at it. Just continue to read the scripts as instructed and the results will come easily.

If your experience matched the description in #2, congratulations to you too! Since you followed the instructions, you most likely hypnotized yourself successfully but you are not yet aware of it. This is normal. Just continue with the method and scripts and the positive results will follow. Most people have no idea they have been hypnotized. Whether you are aware or not, your goals will be reached. And isn't that the best proof?

If you think you experienced nothing, as described in #3, it is very likely you were still successfully hypnotized and didn't know it. Remember hypnosis does not necessarily feel like anything unusual.

To be sure you did everything correctly, here are a few questions to consider:

- Did you carefully follow the preparation and reading instructions?

- Did you read the script slowly?

- Did you follow all the instructions in parentheses?

- Did you use your imagination fully to feel the "warmth of the sun on your skin"? Or to "smell the flowers"? Or to "hear the leaves rustling"?

- Did the reading session take at least 15 minutes? In other words, did you read it slowly enough to absorb it and make it really effective?

If the answer is yes to all of the above, you have done everything correctly and you can expect success.

If the answer is "no" to any of the questions above, please go back and try to read the Master Induction 3.0 again. Just make sure to follow directions this time. Go ahead and do it.

Interesting Hypnotic Phenomena

After you have read Master Induction 3.0 or any of the other inductions included in the next chapter a number of times together with the suggestion script you wish, you might experience some interesting hypnotic symptoms. They might include:

- An unusually deep level of relaxation

- Stumbling or skipping over words or phrases, or inserting words that are not there.

- A "far away feeling" (which is hard to describe but noticeable)

- Changes in your body sensations during the sessions
- Time distortion (e.g., thinking only five minutes has passed by when it's been twenty minutes)
- Waves of emotion rising to your surface of awareness
- The conscious mind thinking of something else distractedly while you continue to read aloud
- Feeling already hypnotized after reading only the first sentence or two
- Euphoria after the session is over, lasting up to many hours (and lots of fun!)

I know these can occur because they have happened to some of my readers and to me. And, the more you read and re-read the hypnotic inductions the more likely you are to encounter some or all of them.

Please note that it is not necessary to experience these things to know you have been hypnotized. They merely indicate certain hypnotic levels may have been achieved. However, deep levels of hypnosis are not required to absorb the post-hypnotic suggestions found in the goal scripts.

Your commitment to do the sessions and your motivation are the two strongest factors required to get results from self hypnosis.

Just be open to the process and be motivated to succeed. Light levels of hypnosis are usually all that is required to get where you want to go anyway.

While very deep levels of hypnosis exist
and may produce bizarre hallucinations,
those levels are not necessary to
achieve results with the 42 scripts.

What Now?

Once you have read the Master Induction 3.0 at least once, it is time to apply the method to one of your goals. In the next chapter, you are given the opportunity to do just that.

INDUCTIONS

The previous chapter introduced you to the self hypnosis as-you-read method but they did not target any of your specific goals. In this chapter, four hypnotic inductions are provided. You will be told how to use them with the 42 self-improvement scripts in the next chapter.

To put the method to work, you first read aloud one of the hypnotic inductions in this chapter. Then turn to the goal script you want and read it out loud. Finish your session by reading The Wake Up to emerge from self hypnosis.

Repeat that procedure once a day, for three to twelve days, or until your results satisfy you.

When you have succeeded with one goal, you may move to another goal script.

Choose Your Induction

One of the most frequent requests I have received is for more induction scripts. People want more variety to keep from getting bored. Fair enough.

Here is why I offered a single induction in my previous books. Reading the same hypnotic induction over and over produces a welcome conditioned response, which makes re-entry into the hypnotic state faster and deeper. I have used the inductions in my previous books so often I enter hypnosis when I read the very first sentence!

As for an induction becoming monotonous, this is not necessarily bad because an interesting phenomenon develops when you get bored while reading aloud. As your conscious mind's attention wanders, another part of your mind—the subconscious—continues to scan and read the script aloud. The conscious filter is bypassed and the words of the script are communicated directly to the subconscious. So, boredom can assist the hypnotic effect. Monotony has its value!

Milton Erickson, an amazing twentieth century hypnotist, became famous for telling long "boring" stories which caused the eyes of his listeners to "glaze" over. That *glazed boredom* produced a hypnotic trance while his stories contained all sorts of suggestions that had a powerful impact on his audiences. My single induction approach in previous books was designed to produce a similar hypnotic effect for my readers.

But to satisfy their requests, I have provided several inductions in this book. Each induction has many things in common but they also have interesting differences that can help induce hypnosis.

Here is an outline of the inductions and how to choose one of them for your session:

- The "Magnificent Mansion Induction" is virtually the same as the Master Induction 3.0 found in the chapter called METHOD. It is also related to Master Induction 2.0 from my book *More Instant Self Hypnosis: Hypnotize Yourself as You Read*, though it has been improved. If you are new to this method or do not know which induction to use, start with the Magnificent Mansion Induction. It works well for a wide variety of personality types.

- The "Downtown Hypnotist Induction" is my personal favorite. It takes the reader to a professional hypnotist's office and induces a receptive state using modern imagery and hidden metaphors to bypass the conscious filter of the mind. This is a great induction if you want an alternative to nature imagery.

- The "Control Center Induction" leads you to relax your body and then imagine entering an electronic science laboratory that connects with your mind and body. If you can see a connection between the body and mind and computers, or if you enjoy science fiction, you will likely respond well to this induction.

- The "Active Progressive Relaxation Induction" guides you through an exercise where you actively tense and re-lax your muscles, one group at a time, while it also calms your mind. This is a great induction if you want to concentrate on releasing stress and anxiety. It is perfect if you do not enjoy imagery because you are not asked to picture or imagine anything.

Note that you may change or alternate inductions from one session to another. In other words, you may use the Control Center Induction for today's session and then decide to use the Downtown Hypnotist Induction script for tomorrow's session and then the Magnificent Mansion the day after tomorrow. It's up to you. All of the inductions work fast and efficiently.

My guess is that you will prefer one or two of the inductions over the others and end up using that favorite(s) exclusively. Feel free to try them all during separate sessions. Experiment and have fun!

Choose and Bookmark A Goal Script

Once you've chosen which induction you would like to use for a session, bookmark it so you can quickly turn to it when you begin.

Next, bookmark a single script in the next chapter that pertains to the goal you want to address. During any one session, you will only be working on one area of change or self-improvement at a time. Many scripts in the next chapter may appeal to you, and eventually you can address all of them. But when it comes to getting results from self hypnosis, it is important to *focus on just one goal topic per session.*

31

To select a goal, look through the script titles offered in the next chapter. They are named in such a way that you should immediately recognize what challenge or topic each addresses. Just beneath each title is a brief description about the script topic. If you are still uncertain whether the script applies to you, read the first few lines of the script and it will be perfectly clear what it is designed to do.

When you have selected an induction script and have bookmarked a goal script in the next chapter, you are ready to begin a self hypnosis session.

Make sure to carefully follow the preparation and reading instructions below before you begin.

Preparation and Reading Instructions

- Find a quiet, comfortable place to read where you will not be disturbed for about 20 minutes.

- Sit in a comfortable chair or sofa where you can relax as you read the script.

- Read the scripts ALOUD.

- While reading the induction, use a relaxed and gentle tone of voice, as if you are reading to calm a young child.

- Read the induction *slowly*.

- You do not need to read the words in parentheses aloud, but follow the directions they contain.

- When directed to pause and imagine something, take the time to do so.

- Pause for a couple of seconds wherever you see three dots (...)

- Pause three to five seconds between each paragraph.

- Emphasize words in italics.

- While reading the suggestions that pertain to your goal, use voice inflection to match the emotional tone of the words.

- Read the entire script in one session, including The Wake Up.

- Repeat the script once a day for three to twelve consecutive days or until you achieve satisfactory results.

Magnificent Mansion Induction

(to be read aloud)

"I hypnotize myself as I read. Right now … I find a quiet and comfortable space where I can easily concentrate on these words as I gently read them aloud.

"With the sound of my voice I can soothe my nervous system … calm my entire body and relax my thoughts. I speak slowly … with a gentle but resonant tone, as though reading a bedtime story to a young child who is getting ready to … go to sleep. The slower I read, the more relaxed the child becomes.

"I make believe everything moves in *slow motion* … (read slower) slow motion … (read even slower) slow motion. And moment by moment, *my mind clears* like the surface of a quiet mountain lake. Clear … calm … quiet.

"I picture myself relaxing in a small and sturdy wooden boat that gently drifts on a glassy lake. The lake is surrounded by tall, stately trees. The sun shines and warms my skin. I fully imagine feeling its golden rays on my body, gently soothing and relaxing me from the top of my head down to the tips of my toes (take a few seconds and imagine this).

"It feels so good that I imagine I close my eyes as I drift on the safe wooden vessel. I listen to the leaves of the trees rustling (pause a moment and imagine you hear the rustling) and I feel a refreshing breeze pass over my body (take a few seconds to see this) … and I smell the sweet scent of wildflowers on the wind (imagine the scent of flowers).

"I am filled with an incredible sense of peace and well-being, as I just allow my mind and the boat to move and drift … carefree … along the mirror-like surface of the serene water. Just drifting now … into gentle pathways of peace and solace ... easily ... effortlessly ... the way I might feel on the border of a sound... deep ... sleep. (read very slowly) *A sound ... deep ... sleep.*

"When I open my eyes I discover the boat has come to a stop upon a lush island. Abundant green plant life looks well cared for as I notice a trail that leads to a magnificent mansion. As I step out of the boat and slowly walk the trail toward the mansion, I *feel mesmerized* by the amazing architecture and grandeur of the great manor.

"I come to a closed iron gate where a formidable-looking guard is standing and looks at me with a steely glare. But that glare quickly turns to a smile because the guard recognizes me and opens the gate saying, 'Welcome home.' I now realize the mansion belongs to me and the guard knows me and works on my behalf.

"I walk through the gate and up to a grand, ornate door on which my own first name is embossed in pure gold. As I speak my name aloud (say your first name aloud) the door opens all by itself, as if by some *mysterious power.* As I step through the threshold of the door, I feel a deep sense of security and well-being.

"There are many hallways and rooms to this mansion representing the many aspects of my mind and my life. I make my way to a short stairway with five stairs that lead down to my favorite thinking place. As I descend the stairs, I count backwards from five to one. As I do, I use my imagination to *relax even deeper* and to glide into a condition of self-hypnosis ... a condition of deep relaxation and heightened receptivity ... with my eyes open.

"Five ... I imagine walking down the stairs and that I feel twice as relaxed with each number.

"Four ... the deeper I go the more open to positive change I now become.

"Three ... effortlessly going deeper down the stairs ... feeling safe and secure yet open and receptive.

"Two ... down into a calm and comfortable place ... where creating positive changes is effortless and uncomplicated.

"One ... at the bottom of the stairs now, and I imagine what it might feel like be in a state of self hypnosis with my eyes open now.

"I enter into a familiar, welcoming reading room. I approach the most comfortable looking chair and sit down to *relax fully*. Feeling peaceful and supported, I pick up a small book on a table next to the chair. I read the cover, with the title that says 'Hypnotize Yourself as You Read.' I open the book and begin to read. The *words speak to me directly* and seem to rise off the pages and into my mind. Here is what they say:

"'You are successfully hypnotized. You are *highly receptive* to positive ideas and suggestions while you remain hypnotized.

"You *remain deeply hypnotized* while you read suggestions corresponding to your purpose and goals. Your mind absorbs and retains desirable suggestions the way a sponge soaks in water. You *easily stay hypnotized* with your eyes open until you finish reading the Wake-Up."

(Turn to your bookmarked goal script and
continue reading.)

Downtown Hypnotist Induction

(to be read aloud)

"To hypnotize myself as I read, I imagine I am on my way to an appointment with an expert hypnotist.

"A trusted friend accompanies me as we casually walk along a city sidewalk. I walk with purpose and notice the pavement pass beneath my feet. (Imagine the sensation of walking on cement.)

"I observe cars, buses, trucks and vans passing by on the street next to me. (Picture city traffic.)

"I hear the sounds of traffic and car horns. (Imagine the sound of car horns.)

"I smell the city air. There's a delicious scent from a nearby food truck, but also the slight scent of car exhaust. (Sniff the air and imagine smelling this.)

"My friend asks me why I want to be hypnotized. I say it is because hypnosis will provide me a way to improve myself and get what I want. My friend can think of no objections and we continue on our way.

"In a short time we reach the right address and walk into a building with stunning architecture, decor and colors I love and appreciate. An attendant at the main desk informs me that the hypnotist's office is located down the escalator.

"My friend and I step onto a deep, long escalator which immediately begins to take us down toward the lower level. The ride of the escalator is so quiet, smooth and *soothing* that my friend looks very sleepy and yawns several times.

"The deeper we descend, the *more relaxed* we feel. Deeper down we glide toward the level below the surface.

We consider with amusement whether the *relaxing escalator ride* might hypnotize us before we even reach the hypnotist.

"At last we reach the bottom of the escalator and step off of it. This lower level has a different look and feel than the level above, but I like it even more because it makes me *feel relaxed.*

"The large door of the hypnotist's office is just ahead. I knock three times.(Imagine hearing the sound of knocking on a door three times.)

"The hypnotist answers the door and appears exactly how I would imagine a hypnotist might look. (Pretend how the hypnotist looks.)

- "I am invited into the office, but the hypnotist politely says to my friend, 'You will have to wait out here. Just relax and we will be finished in a short while.' My friend agrees and sits down in a plush chair just outside the door.

"I step inside the office which is cozy and warmly decorated. The hypnotist closes the door and it feels like we are in a private world where deep things are discussed and solutions are found. I am asked why I have come for hypnosis and the reasons why it's important that I succeed.

(Pause fifteen seconds as you think about
why you want to succeed.)

"The hypnotist nods and says, 'Those are excellent reasons, so I know you are going to do very well with hypnosis today.'

"We sit down in comfortable chairs facing one another and the hypnotist says, 'If you do what I ask of you, then you will easily and automatically be hypnotized. Listen to the sound of my *hypnotic voice.* I am going to count slowly backwards from ten to one and you will relax deeper with each number. Your body will relax deeper and your mind will relax deeper. Are you ready and willing to do that?'

"I agree and nod.

(Read the following VERY slowly.)

"The hypnotist smiles and says, 'Good. All you have to do is want it to happen and you can make it happen very easily.

"10...notice your feet and legs feeling heavy and relaxed now.

"9...feel your buttocks, abdomen and solar plexus becoming calm and comfortable.

"8... your chest...your back...and your shoulders loosen and relax. Loosen and relax.

"7... your upper arms and lower arms relax twice as deeply as before.

"6...and your hands and fingers relax so completely now that you might even feel a change in sensation, such as a tingling or a warmth.

"5...the back of your neck feels loose and flexible.

"4...your jaw and the muscles of your cheeks and around your eyes become slack.

"3... and your brow and scalp relax.

"2...your whole body from the top of your head down to the soles of your feet are more relaxed than ever before.

"1...your mind is clear, relaxed and perfectly receptive to hypnotic suggestions that will change your life for the better. Do you feel relaxed and receptive now?

"Feeling as though I am in a very deep hypnotic trance, I reply, 'Yes.'

"Good. You can return to this level of relaxation and receptivity quickly and easily anytime you wish whenever you listen to these words again.

"I'm now going to place before you a series of hypnotic suggestions so you can get exactly what you came to accomplish today. As you read each suggestion, you completely absorb the meaning into your mind and body. Think of how happy you feel as you consider the ways your life is about to change. When you have read the suggestions for your goal, you will then read *The Wake Up* to return yourself to the everyday state of mind."

(Turn to the script you want and
continue reading aloud.)

Control Room Induction

(to be read aloud)

"Whether I am ready to become hypnotized at this moment or later on, I reserve a quiet time and place now … so I can relax while I comfortably concentrate on this hypnotic script.

"As I read these words out loud, I speak in a soothing and harmonious tone, as if I was using my voice to hypnotize someone in the room. I read slowly and I now begin to sense my relaxation deepening.

"I keep my eyes open just enough to take in the *following words.*

"I let my eyes blink naturally when they want to … and they might start to feel heavy and droopy … the way they feel as I read a book before going to sleep. I use my imagination so that with every word I read I become more relaxed and drowsier. (imagine feeling drowsy) My eyes remain open as I get more calm now … like a peaceful sea after a storm.

"I turn my attention to my breathing, and use this opportunity to relax my mind and my body more deeply.

"As I count my out-breaths backwards from ten to one, I let each number represent a gradually deeper level of relaxation. I use my imagination to relax twice as deeply with each number and with each exhalation.

(Draw a breath before reading each number, and count as you exhale.)

"Ten … I double my relaxation …

"Nine … with every number and every breath.

"Eight ... I count slowly as I go deeper ... *deeper still.*

"Seven ... I use my imagination to double my relaxation.

"Six ... with each number and exhalation it doubles.

"Five ... I let myself enjoy ...

"Four ... this relaxing experience ...

"Three ... so very deeply.

"Two ... and I look forward to the benefits ...

"One ... of self hypnosis.

(Pause for five seconds and
breathe normally.)

"At this *deeper level,* people experience different things. Some notice interesting body sensations ... such as a tingling in their fingers. I might also have that *experience.*

(Pause five seconds.)

"Some feel a floating sensation ... with a dreamy quality. I may experience that.

(Pause five seconds.)

"Whatever sensations I experience are exactly right for me at this moment. Whether I feel something unusual now or at some other time, I let that process happen on its own.

"I now imagine walking down the corridor of a futuristic science facility. At the end of the hall is a secure, white door marked CONTROL CENTER. To open the door, I place my hand on a special fingerprint ID pad on the door. Then an automated voice says: 'Welcome', and calls me by name to come inside.

"The door slides open, and I observe a room full of advanced computers and instruments. There are many monitors revealing flowing data. There is a hologram showing my full body. And I am amazed to realize that I am in the control center of *my own mind and body*.

"In the middle of the room, I see a futuristic grey chair on a lighted pedestal. I step onto the pedestal and I sit down. An unusual electronic helmet lowers automatically and rests on the crown of my head. A large screen flashes as it reads: YOU ARE NOW READY TO INPUT AND ABSORB SUGGESTIONS TO OPTIMIZE YOUR LIFE. PRESS *PROGRAMMING* ON THE CHAIR TO BEGIN NOW.

"I press a button that reads PROGRAMMING. It lights up and I feel a surging connection between the helmet and my mind and body.

"The following suggestions then appear on the screen in front of me. And I read them to input new information for my mind and body to process and assimilate...."

(Turn to the goal script of your choice and
continue reading aloud.)

Active Progressive Relaxation Induction

(to be read aloud)

"I hypnotize myself with my eyes open as I read this script and follow the instructions it contains.

"I speak slowly and softly with a relaxed tone of voice ... and the sound of my own voice soothes my mind and body. With every word I speak I feel *more deeply relaxed*. And the more relaxed I feel, the *more receptive I am* to all life-changing suggestions I read during this session.

"To help me relax as deeply as possible, I choose to release all unnecessary tension from my body and my mind. Because when my *body is relaxed*, my *thoughts relax*. And when my thoughts relax, *my body relaxes*. And when they are both relaxed, it is easy for me to absorb life-changing suggestions.

"I will concentrate on relaxing one body part at a time, starting with my feet and progressing to my head. By tensing and releasing these parts, I automatically relax my body and my mind deeper.

"I place my attention on my feet and tense all of the muscles there for the count of three.

(Tense both feet while counting.)

"One ... two ... three.

"Now I relax all of the muscles of my feet completely. (Relax feet muscles.) I let my feet just *rest comfortably* ... and as I do, I feel safe and secure.

"Next, I place my awareness on my lower leg muscles, the calf muscles. To the best of my ability, I *isolate and gently contract* the calf muscles for the count of three.

(Tense the calves while counting.)

"One ... two ... three.

(Now relax the calf muscles.)

"I now *release all tension* in my lower legs. I let them rest deeper and deeper as now move my focus to my upper legs.

"I contract the muscles of my upper legs for the slow count of three.

(Tense the upper legs.)

"One ... two ... three.

(Release the upper leg muscles.)

"I *release all stress* now from my upper legs. They are completely at ease and I let life carry me as I shift my thoughts to my buttocks.

"Right where I am sitting, I tighten my butt firmly as I count...

(Tense the buttocks.)

"One ... two ... three.

"And with the number three I relax the muscles of the buttocks as I feel that all is well.

"Now I move my concentration to my stomach muscles and tense them as I count.

(Tense stomach muscles.)

"One … two … three.

(Relax the stomach.)

"I effortlessly release my stomach muscles and process life with ease.

"And as I count, I gently tighten my chest muscles…

"One … two … three.

(Relax the chest.)

"As I fully relax my chest, I also relax any thoughts that were weighing on me. I let them go now and feel lighter.

"I now tense my shoulders as I count by lifting them in a shrug.

(Tense the shoulders, lifting them
toward the ears in a shrug.)

"One … two … three.

(Release the shoulders by letting them drop.)

"I release my shoulders as I also relax all thoughts about my responsibilities and handle all things with joy.

"And finally, I focus my awareness on my face and head and hold a tight expression as I count…

(Tense the mouth and brow and tighten the jaw, in a scowl.)

"One ... two ... three.

(Relax the face and brow.)

"And now I relax and loosen all of the muscles of my face ... my jaw ... my brow ... and express relaxed thoughts and emotions.

"I draw and release three slow deep breaths as I count them...

(Draw a breath and release it.)

"One ... twice as deeply relaxed with each out-breath...

(Draw a breath and exhale.)

"Two ... more relaxed than ever before ...

(Draw a breath and release it.)

"Three ... I feel in synch with the rhythms of my body and mind.

"I am now hypnotized with my eyes open. I am ready to read and receive the positive suggestions for my goal. I embrace the hypnotic suggestions and absorb them into my mind and body so that they will bestow immediate and lasting benefits for my life. And I remain hypnotized now as I continue to read...."

(Turn to the goal script of your choice and
continue reading aloud.)

SCRIPTS

The 42 scripts in this chapter contain post-hypnotic suggestions related to specific life goals.

The scripts are named in a way to easily identify the challenge they address. Beneath each title is a very brief description. If you are uncertain if a script applies to you, read through the script before doing the induction to decide whether the suggestions are appropriate to your circumstances.

When you have selected the script topic for your session, bookmark it.

Begin the session by reading one of the bookmarked inductions offered in the previous chapter. Then click the bookmarked goal script and continue to read aloud.

Finish each session by slowly reading The Wake Up script completely. It is provided at the end of each goal script, no bookmarking necessary.

Perpetual Stress Relief

This script will help relieve ongoing stress due to today's busy and stressful lifestyle.

"I experience increased freedom from perpetual stress and anxiety.

"Through the power of self hypnosis I break the cycle of perpetual stress and direct my subconscious mind to relax my nervous system and the muscles of my body.

"I imagine myself wrapped in a deep blue blanket of relaxation and tranquility. I picture it around my entire body, from my head to my toes so that only my face is showing.

(Take 15 seconds and
fully imagine it.)

"I feel safe and secure covered in the soft, cozy blanket. I feel like a baby being cared for by a strong and protective guardian. Like a happy and well-loved infant, I feel utterly supported, peaceful and completely worry-free now. All is well.

"And now I picture the deep blue blanket's color as liquid light that not only surrounds me, but also fills every part of my being.

(Take 15 seconds to imagine
the blue light filling you.)

"My breathing becomes more relaxed and regular now. My heartbeat slows down to a safe and comfortable rhythm. My muscles and nerve endings are calm and tension-free.

My thoughts are gentle and quiet. My feelings are those of bliss and deep serenity.

"In this timeless moment, all is well. I am safe. I am supported. I am at peace. I can relax. I can let go. Right now.

(Take a full 30 seconds to
experience calm.)

"After I emerge from this self hypnosis session, I will continue to feel safe, supported and peaceful. I will feel as though a heavy weight around my body and mind has dropped away. And what remains is a calm and centered state of being.

"With every passing day, this calm and centered way of thinking and feeling becomes my natural way of being.

"If I ever notice myself feeling unnecessary tension or stress, I will say to myself, 'Calm and centered.' When I say that phrase, it triggers a relaxation response throughout my body and mind. I will instantly feel relaxed and safe.

"As a result of releasing perpetual stress, I am free to rediscover the happiness I feel deep within. It is as though I was encased in a giant ice cube. The warm and healing sunlight melted the ice, freeing my body and soul and allowing me to come alive. All that was left of the ice cube was a puddle, which has now evaporated completely.

"I am free to enjoy my life now and in the future."

(The Wake-Up)

"I will emerge gently and easily from hypnosis now by counting from one to five. With each number I emerge twenty percent. When I reach the number five, I will return to everyday awareness.

"One . . . emerging twenty percent, beginning to awaken from hypnosis now. (Speak a little louder and stronger.)

"Two . . . forty percent now, as I become fully aware of my body and environment. (Speak louder and stronger.)

"Three . . . sixty percent . . . I look forward to positive results from this hypnosis session. (Speak louder and stronger.)

"Four . . . eighty percent, emerging peaceful and happy. (Strongly assert your intention to emerge.)

"FIVE . . . FIVE . . . FIVE . . . One hundred percent now! Wide awake and fully alert!!!"

Drop the Last Ten Pounds

This script helps people who struggle to lose the final pounds achieve their ideal weight.

"I drop the last ten pounds of excess fat and weight.

"It is time to get serious and focus on letting go of the last ten pounds I want to drop. With absolute resolve and the help of self hypnosis, I move forward with my intention and achieve my weight goal.

"While I am pleased that I am only ten pounds from my ideal weight, I am not yet completely satisfied. I now decide to accelerate my weight loss plan to reach my ultimate goal. I plan to weigh ten pounds less … to look and feel ten pounds leaner. I do everything in my power *to safely release* the last ten pounds of body weight. I let nothing and no one stop me from a feeling of full satisfaction.

"I call upon my subconscious to safely *boost my metabolism* to a rate most effective for burning fat and releasing weight. It is as though my body is a car that has been in low gear. But now I am shifting into high gear so that I can burn fuel faster, have more energy and reach my destination sooner. And when I reach the finish line, the last ten pounds I want to lose are gone!

"Because my body goes into a higher gear and provides me with *more energy*, I feel a strong urge to move my body through exercise and athletic activity. Not only do I discover how good it feels to energetically move my body, I also feel good because the vigorous movement helps me to reach my intended goal weight quickly. So I am motivated to *become physically active*.

"Until I *reach my goal*, I consume only foods and beverages that align with my goal to drop the final ten pounds. I eliminate all other or excessive amounts of food or caloric beverages from my eating pattern. And with the help of my subconscious I realize I don't even want them anymore. They don't appeal to me, because consuming them doesn't make me happy.

"What does make me happy is enjoying a lighter, tighter body. What makes me happy is dropping the last ten pounds of excess weight ... once and for all!

"I imagine the exact number of pounds or kilos I want to weigh ... the exact number I will weigh ... when I lose the final ten pounds. Even with my eyes open I picture that number flashing in large red numerals. (Pause and picture it for five seconds.)

"As I think of that weight and that number, I experience great happiness and anticipation. I realize that my goal is achievable and that letting go of the last ten pounds is easily within my power to achieve.

"It is like I have been in a long, steady race and now I see the finish line is only ten short steps ahead. I am excited to see the finish line, so I push myself now to go faster so that I can complete the race. And as I get closer and closer, I feel better and better, because I have accomplished something I set out to do.

"When I have dropped the last ten pounds I will celebrate my victory. I reward myself. Whether it is a new article of clothing or a day at the spa, or anything else I want, I treat myself to it because I have earned it. By dropping the last ten pounds, I not only feel good about my body, I also *feel more confident* than ever. And that is worth celebrating!"

(The Wake-Up)

"I will emerge gently and easily from hypnosis now by counting from one to five. With each number I emerge twenty

percent. When I reach the number five, I will return to everyday awareness.

"One . . . emerging twenty percent, beginning to awaken from hypnosis now. (Speak a little louder and stronger.)

"Two . . . forty percent now, as I become fully aware of my body and environment. (Speak louder and stronger.)

"Three . . . sixty percent . . . I look forward to positive results from this hypnosis session. (Speak louder and stronger.)

"Four . . . eighty percent, emerging peaceful and happy. (Strongly assert your intention to emerge.)

"FIVE . . . FIVE . . . FIVE . . . One hundred percent now! Wide awake and fully alert!!!"

Let Go of the Baby Weight

This script will help women lose the weight they gained during pregnancy.

"I let go of any weight I gained before my pregnancy.

"With a strong determination and the help of self hypnosis, I commit to releasing the weight I gained as a result of pregnancy. Day by day, I lose ounces, pounds and inches until I return to the weight and the figure I had before I was pregnant.

"It is natural and healthy for some women to put on extra pounds during pregnancy. And, because it is natural, I release myself from any blame or self-criticism about weight I gained. I can smile at myself and say, 'That's normal.' I appreciate all that goes into being pregnant, giving birth and being a mother.

"However, I now choose to take 100% responsibility for the condition of my body and my weight. It is time to get my body back in shape so I can look and feel the way I want.

"I recognize that any excuses that some women make for remaining overweight are merely rationalizations masquerading as truth. The truth is that anyone can lose weight when they put their mind to it. Therefore, I set my mind to letting go of the baby weight.

"And because I remain faithful to my commitment to release the baby weight, my deep mind helps me succeed faster and easier with the help of self hypnosis.

"I program my mind now to *eat less food*. Now that I am no longer pregnant, I let go of fattening foods. I return to eating moderate portions of healthy food so that I return to my former weight.

"I easily recall how I used to eat before I was pregnant. There was no need or desire for excess calories. There were no cravings for particular foods. As my mind and body remember that way of eating, I can choose to eat less again ... and that idea appeals to me. As I eat light, I automatically feel lighter, slimmer and sexier. And it feels so good to feel that way again that there is no way I would ever return to eating the way I did when I was pregnant. I want to express myself as a healthy, active woman who takes care of herself and who exudes self-confidence. Eating light allows me to express myself that way. It allows me to see myself not just as a mother, but also as an attractive woman.

"And now that I am no longer pregnant, I have an increasing urge to *move my body more* through walking or other exercise. The movement connects me with my body and reminds me that I am alive, so I take great pleasure in moving my body. It is something I look forward to doing as part of my regular lifestyle.

"As I *eat lighter* and move my body more, the pounds and inches begin to melt away. Day by day I lose the baby weight and return my body to the shape I desire. *I feel good about myself.*

"I imagine seeing how my body will look just a couple of months from today and how the baby weight has come off. I like what I see in the mirror. As I gaze at my reflection, a surge or pride in my accomplishment fills me. I realize I can change my body and my life in definite and remarkable ways. I see myself slip on a dress I could not wear because of the gained pregnancy weight. And now it fits perfectly again.

"But losing the weight is about much more than just looking good. As I gaze at my reflection, a surge or pride in my accomplishment fills me. I realize I can change my body and my life in definite and remarkable ways.

"As I eat light and move my body more, my hormones and metabolism return to levels perfect for losing excess fat.

My body chemistry now matches my desire to release the baby weight and reshape my body.

"Whenever I sit down with a plate of food from now on, I will discover that I feel satisfied after eating just a few bites. As I see the remaining food on my plate I ask myself, 'Will eating more help me feel good about myself?' If the answer is Yes, then I can choose to eat the remaining food. If the answer is No, then I lose all interest in eating any more of the food in front of me.

"After this self hypnosis session is over, my desire and motivation to drop the baby weight will increase hour by hour, day by day, until I am pleased and satisfied with the health and appearance of my body.

"It feels good to take control of my body once again ... to move forward with the confidence that I can change and improve my body, and return to an ideal and healthy weight for me."

(The Wake-Up)

"I will emerge gently and easily from hypnosis now by counting from one to five. With each number I emerge twenty percent. When I reach the number five, I will return to everyday awareness.

"One . . . emerging twenty percent, beginning to awaken from hypnosis now. (Speak a little louder and stronger.)

"Two . . . forty percent now, as I become fully aware of my body and environment. (Speak louder and stronger.)

"Three . . . sixty percent . . . I look forward to positive results from this hypnosis session. (Speak louder and stronger.)

"Four . . . eighty percent, emerging peaceful and happy. (Strongly assert your intention to emerge.)

"FIVE . . . FIVE . . . FIVE . . . One hundred percent now! Wide awake and fully alert!!!"

Social Anxiety Relief

This script helps you feel at ease before and during social situations.

"I choose to feel relaxed and comfortable before and during all social situations and occasions.

"Through the power of self-hypnosis, I reprogram my mind and body to feel relaxed and comfortable before and during all social situations and to see myself as a social person.

"I dissolve all fears about being social as I acknowledge that those fears are imaginary. They are not based on reality.

"I once worried how I might appear to others, and I imagined that people might not like me or approve of me or accept me. The imaginary thoughts turned into anxious feelings, and I avoided being social and connecting with others. To rationalize my fears, I might have told myself that I am not a social person or that I don't need people to be happy. But that also is imaginary and untrue.

"I choose now to break through the imaginary cage of fear and solitude I have created. I want to *feel relaxed and social* so I can be more happy and successful in my personal and professional life.

"I choose to believe that people like me and approve of me. I enjoy the company of other people, whether they are friends, family, associates or even strangers.

"I replace the lie I told myself about being a loner. I replace it with the truth that I am a *social person*. While it is perfectly acceptable to enjoy periods alone, I recognize that all human beings are social creatures. Interacting with fellow human beings is healthy, stimulating and brings greater happiness and fulfillment. I accept and embrace that I am a *social person* with social needs and desires. With every passing day I think I am a more healthy, happy and social human being.

"From now on, I think of myself as friendly and approachable.

"I replace imaginary fears by imagining something better … about how others perceive me. I choose to imagine that others like me just as I am. They like the way I look. They like the way I talk. They like the way I act.

"From now on, before and after any social occasion, I choose to believe that people like and respect me. And as I imagine that people think well of me, I feel a wonderful sense of freedom to enjoy participating in social events.

"I am well liked by everyone at social events.

"I imagine standing on the inside of a small, gray prison cell. It is very cold, musty and lonely. I hear noise and laughter coming from beyond the cell. I look through the small barred window of the cell door and see a warm and inviting room of people having a party. They are engaged in conversation and enjoying their company. As I feel a sense of desire and determination to *join the party,* I reach for the cell door to see if it's locked. My hand passes right through the door, and I realize the door and the cell are not real. They are illusions I have created!

"As I remind myself that I want and deserve to enjoy myself socially, the gray cell disappears entirely and I am free to enjoy the party. As I move forward a few steps, I feel that others can now see me and they greet me with warm smiles. They welcome me into their circle of conversation. They ask me how I am doing. They are interested in my opinions about many things. They find me interesting and personable. And it is a marvelous feeling to I connect with others.

"Approaching and speaking to people is easier for me now, because just as I was once concerned about what people might think of me, I realize that others care much more about what I think of them. They want me to like them and accept them too. So we are all equals!

"I remain myself at all times. And I show genuine interest in anyone I encounter.

"Eye contact is an easy way to improve a connection with someone. Therefore, I take opportunities to make comfortable eye contact with anyone I communicate with in person. When I am questioned about something, I offer my opinion freely. When other people talk, I pay attention and nod to them occasionally to acknowledge I understand them. And, as I show other people courtesy and respect in conversation, they do the same for me.

"I relax before and during all social gatherings. Whenever I am invited to any social gathering, I immediately repeat the phrase to myself, '*I look forward to that.*' When I repeat that phrase, I remember I am a social creature and look forward to being with other people.

"As I prepare to enter any social gathering or meeting, I remember that I have dissolved the imaginary wall between me and others. I can feel free to join in conversations and share myself with others. I can allow others to share themselves with me.

"If I ever feel anxious or tense before any social gathering, I draw a deep breath as I tense my shoulders, pulling them up toward my head. As I do this, I furrow my brow and feel all the pressure...all the worry...all the anxiety...that I've placed on myself *(perform this action now)*.

"As I release the breath *(release the breath)*, I also let my shoulders drop and release all tension in my face and brow *(relax the face and shoulders)*. And as I do that, I imagine I've released all of the pressure...all the worry...all the anxiety...that I once placed on myself. I say to myself now '*Social and comfortable.*'

"I repeat that to myself once, twice or three times until I feel my body, my emotions and my thoughts becoming comfortable and calm. When I am finished, I feel just *fine about the social gathering* and look forward to *interacting with people.*

"And because the pressure is off . . . I can allow myself to simply connect with people and let them respond to me naturally. From now on, I choose to relax in all social situations whether with friends, acquaintances or strangers. As I feel calm and comfortable in any conversation, my mind and memory works normally and beautifully and I speak with poise and clarity.

"I socially connect with people with ease and poise."

(The Wake-Up)

"I will emerge gently and easily from hypnosis now by counting from one to five. With each number I emerge twenty percent. When I reach the number five, I will return to everyday awareness.

"One . . . emerging twenty percent, beginning to awaken from hypnosis now. (Speak a little louder and stronger.)

"Two . . . forty percent now, as I become fully aware of my body and environment. (Speak louder and stronger.)

"Three . . . sixty percent . . . I look forward to positive results from this hypnosis session. (Speak louder and stronger.)

"Four . . . eighty percent, emerging peaceful and happy. (Strongly assert your intention to emerge.)

"FIVE . . . FIVE . . . FIVE . . . One hundred percent now! Wide awake and fully alert!!!"

Money Stress Relief

This script will help lessen physical and mental stress caused by money concerns.

"I relieve stress and control feelings related to money challenges.

"I acknowledge money challenges and responsibilities. I accept my financial issues as well as the fear and anger I feel about them. By acknowledging the challenges, I stop resisting reality. As I stop resisting or denying the way things are, I *start to breathe easier* and completely accept the situation. Anger and fear now begin to dissolve and vanish entirely.

"I totally and *completely forgive myself* for these money challenges. The fear and frustration I've experienced are understandable. Most people experience money troubles many times during their lives. And they have felt the same kind of anxiety and frustration I have experienced. So this is a natural human problem and a natural human reaction.

"As I *forgive myself* for having these challenges and for any negative reactions to them, I already *start to feel better.* I extend the same compassion to myself as I would to anyone else with money challenges. The compassion I offer myself soothes and heals my body and mind.

"I *release fears* about my life and circumstances based on an imaginary future. Many of the stressful feelings about my financial issues come from my imagination running away with me. Without realizing it, I may have been imagining extreme and unpleasant things about the future if these challenges were not resolved. But the truth is that these unpleasant things have not happened yet, so I choose to stop myself from predicting negative events and circumstances. As I do that and remain positive about the future, my body and mind relax as stressful feelings evaporate like mist on a warm, sunny day.

"I choose, instead, to imagine a time in the near future when I have already overcome and resolved the money problems. I picture myself with enough money in my bank account to easily pay all my bills. I see a surplus of currency coming to me from expected and unexpected sources. I picture myself cashing large checks payable in my name. And I feel a sense of happiness and pride in overcoming my money challenges. I realize now that I have become stronger as a result of those very money problems. Now, I am able to face troubles confidently while I remain calm.

"I bring peace and composure to my mind and body now by realizing I am safe at this moment. As I take three slow deep breaths now, I assure my body I am safe here and now (take three slow deep breaths). Here and now there is no danger. While stress is a wonderful survival response in times of danger, there is no physical threat right now. I'm *perfectly okay* at this moment. By reminding myself I'm safe and comfortable right now, I allow my muscles and nervous system to deeply relax.

"As I work through my financial challenges, I anticipate solutions to resolve and move beyond them. Some of these solutions will naturally present themselves to me as I move forward. Solutions may come from expected or unexpected people and sources. As I search for answers, I feel comfortable asking individuals, institutions and organizations for help or compassion. We all need help in our lives from time to time. This is part of the human experience.

"And now that I feel more relaxed, I affirm that I can and I will handle any and all financial difficulties with patience, dignity and intelligence. I will find resources to help overcome those challenges. I see and think of myself as strong, responsible and self-aware. I move forward to handle my circumstances with money while I remember how strong and resourceful I am."

(The Wake-Up)

"I will emerge gently and easily from hypnosis now by counting from one to five. With each number I emerge twenty percent. When I reach the number five, I will return to everyday awareness.

"One . . . emerging twenty percent, beginning to awaken from hypnosis now. (Speak a little louder and stronger.)

"Two . . . forty percent now, as I become fully aware of my body and environment. (Speak louder and stronger.)

"Three . . . sixty percent . . . I look forward to positive results from this hypnosis session. (Speak louder and stronger.)

"Four . . . eighty percent, emerging peaceful and happy. (Strongly assert your intention to emerge.)

"FIVE . . . FIVE . . . FIVE . . . One hundred percent now! Wide awake and fully alert!!!"

Manifest a New Job

This script will assist you to seek and manifest employment.

"I manifest a new job.

"Through the power of self hypnosis I tap the resources of my mind to manifest a job I enjoy and which pays me well.

"From the unlimited riches of energy and thought, I direct my subconscious to draw to me the people and circumstances I need to secure a wonderful new job.

"I dissolve all fear and disappointment related to previous employment or employers. I release the past. I concentrate on the here and now. I plan to seek and find new work so I may enjoy my life to a greater degree than ever.

"Today is a day I have never experienced. I consider there are opportunities available today that were not available yesterday. As I summon these opportunities to me and seek them out, I attract a job that meets or exceeds my expectations.

"Starting now, deep wells of motivation to seek new employment arise in me. This motivation doubles every morning when I wake up until my new position is secured. I feel determined now to contact employers and arrange job interviews. I have a deep and abiding sense that I will find the new job I am looking for. As I actively seek a new job, it feels like that job is waiting for me to discover it. And the more I look for that new job, the sooner I connect with it.

"A new job is available and waiting for me. I claim it for myself now. I manifest a new job.

"I contemplate what having a new job that I enjoy might look and feel like. I consider what kind of work I would like to do: ... the appearance and temperament of my work associates ... the way my workspace looks ... and the amount of money that goes into my bank account when I get paid.

(Take a minute and imagine the kind of work and place you want to manifest.)

"I see myself walking through a door to a building and interviewing for a job with a potential employer. I am poised and articulate as we discuss the details of the job and my qualifications for it. I show enthusiasm and interest about the prospect of working for this company while I remain confident and relaxed. The interviewer tells me that they will call if they want to hire me. Then I give thanks for the interview, walk out of the building and feel good about how I presented myself.

"I continue to search with expectation and enthusiasm no matter how many jobs I apply for. The more jobs I apply for the better I feel.

"I imagine standing in front of a locked modern door made of gold. Next to me is a chest full of keys of all different appearances. . I take out a key and attempt to put it into the lock of the door. But this key is too small. I pull out of the chest another key and try it. This key is too wide. My intuition informs me that the right key is in the chest and that it is just a matter of time before I *find the one that fits*. After trying each key that does not fit, I feel better and better, because I am eliminating the wrong keys and zeroing in on the right one.

"At last I pull a very special key from the chest. The size and weight of it appeal to me and it appears to be just right. I slip the key into the lock and turn it. I hear the tumblers turn, and I realize that I have unlocked the door!

"I open the gold door, and on the other side I see the most beautiful mountain sunrise I could ever imagine. My determination and persistence has paid off!

"I actively and relentlessly seek the manifestation of a new job. The more I seek it, the closer I come to the right job for me at this time.

"I now attract the right job for me. And I look forward to its full manifestation."

(The Wake-Up)

"I will emerge gently and easily from hypnosis now by counting from one to five. With each number I emerge twenty percent. When I reach the number five, I will return to everyday awareness.

"One . . . emerging twenty percent, beginning to awaken from hypnosis now. (Speak a little louder and stronger.)

"Two . . . forty percent now, as I become fully aware of my body and environment. (Speak louder and stronger.)

"Three . . . sixty percent . . . I look forward to positive results from this hypnosis session. (Speak louder and stronger.)

"Four . . . eighty percent, emerging peaceful and happy. (Strongly assert your intention to emerge.)

"FIVE . . . FIVE . . . FIVE . . . One hundred percent now! Wide awake and fully alert!!!"

Save More Money

This script will help you to conserve money to accumulate wealth.

"I conserve and save more money.

"I develop a *money-saving mindset* so I *accumulate more wealth.* I appreciate the value of money and dissolve childlike desires for immediate gratification. As I freely choose to spend less money on a daily, weekly and monthly basis, I *automatically save more money.* The more I save, the more money becomes available for financial security and for things I want and need. Those *things I wanted are worth patiently saving for.*

"I take *control of my spending habits now.* I accept and embrace the mature responsibility of handling my money wisely. And as I do that I discover I am quite good at saving money. I realize that saving money makes me feel like a powerful and responsible adult, because responsible adults take charge of their finances. They decide carefully before spending money and they *save money whenever possible.*

"From this day forward I become acutely aware of my purchasing behavior. As my awareness increases, my freedom to change my behavior also increases. So as I observe myself about to spend money on anything at all, I have a window of opportunity *to rethink the purchase.* I *carefully consider all of my purchases,* both large and small, because I know that every dollar I put aside contributes to my happiness and well-being.

"My subconscious mind automatically prompts me to save money whenever and wherever possible. As I consider any expenditure, this question will arise in my mind, 'Do I really need to spend my money on this?' When it arises, my mind becomes clear of emotional bias so that I can *evaluate rationally*.

"If the expenditure is wise or necessary, I continue the transaction confidently. If I determine the expense is unwise or frivolous, I immediately discontinue the transaction and feel a surge of satisfaction that I have saved money.

"I imagine myself wheeling a shopping cart in a grocery store. I have a list of items I need to purchase. As I walk down the aisle, I see many food and beverages with colorful, attractive packaging. As I reach for a product that is not on my list, the question comes quickly to my mind: 'Do I really need to spend my money on this?' My thinking instantly becomes clear and free from emotional impulses. I decide the product is not on my list and is, therefore, unnecessary. I put the frivolous product back on the shelf and feel a wave of pride and satisfaction. I discover that this freedom and self-control feels much better than purchasing a thing I don't need. And I realize that saving money is fun!

"Whether it's cutting out coupons or waiting for sales, I seek ways to save money. Even millionaires seek good sales and bargains, so saving money in no way makes me a miser or a cheapskate. Saving money makes me smart and responsible. The more money I save, the more I can choose to spend on family, friends or charities if that's what I want. The more money I save, the more generous I can be without harming my financial well-being.

"I imagine myself a month from now as I review my bank account statement. I notice the reduction of expenditures and a modest increase in the balance. I have taken a positive step toward a secure and better future and that feels good. It makes me want to save even more money in the months that follow.

"Now I pretend a year has passed and I feel positively elated as I review my bank statement. The account balance is higher than it has ever been and I realize that I have amassed a sizable amount of money. I am filled with a sense of financial security and freedom. I now have a greater abundance of money and I am proud of myself for saving it. The money is there to serve me however I choose. I even consider saving up for something I have wanted for a long time and it feels so good to know I have the mindset of a saver.

"I realize I would never exchange these feelings of financial well-being and security back for careless and frivolous spending. No way! I want to keep feeling the pride and happiness that saving and accumulating money give me. So I will continue to save money whenever and wherever possible.

"When this self hypnosis session ends in a few moments, I will emerge with a money-saving mindset. The old devil-may-care attitudes and behaviors about money will be gone and in their place will be feelings of self-control and power. Because saving more money not only makes me feel good about my finances, it makes me feel good about myself. And when I feel good about myself, I experience the kind of wealth that comes from deep within and brings me true satisfaction."

(The Wake-Up)

"I will emerge gently and easily from hypnosis now by counting from one to five. With each number I emerge twenty percent. When I reach the number five, I will return to everyday awareness.

"One . . . emerging twenty percent, beginning to awaken from hypnosis now. (Speak a little louder and stronger.)

"Two . . . forty percent now, as I become fully aware of my body and environment. (Speak louder and stronger.)

"Three . . . sixty percent . . . I look forward to positive results from this hypnosis session. (Speak louder and stronger.)

"Four . . . eighty percent, emerging peaceful and happy. (Strongly assert your intention to emerge.)

"FIVE . . . FIVE . . . FIVE . . . One hundred percent now! Wide awake and fully alert!!!"

Get Over Your Ex

This script will help you let go of emotional attachment and pain from a previous intimate relationship.

"I am ready to get over a previous relationship and move on with my life.

"It was good and healthy for me to take time to recover after my relationship ended. But it is time to heal now and let that relationship slip into the past where it belongs so I may experience full joy in my life in the present and future.

"With the help of self hypnosis, I give myself permission to emotionally mend so I can *look forward to the happiness waiting for me.*

"I release all mental and emotional attachments to my ex and our former relationship. It is time to cut the cord of regret and stop the wishful thinking about my ex, and to make room in my life for other relationships..

"I picture myself with my ex on a sandy beach ending our relationship and saying goodbye. As we turn our backs and walk in opposite directions, I imagine that there is an elastic rope extending from my solar plexus that is attached to the solar plexus of my ex. Even though we walk farther and farther away from each other, the elastic rope keeps me tethered to my ex.

"Sometimes I feel a tug pulling me back a few feet toward my ex, and it is impairing my movement forward. It is time to make a clean break.

"So I now imagine taking a large pair of silver scissors and I cut the cord of attachment to my ex. Surprisingly, it cuts cleanly and easily and then the rope disappears completely.

The attachment has been severed. And I *feel free to walk in a new direction.*

"I notice a group of people having a party on the beach. They invite me to join them. As I join in the festivities, I enjoy these new friends and get involved. I look forward to meeting new friends and moving on to the next phase of my life.

"With every hour and day that follows this session, the thought of my ex becomes more of a distant memory. It seems as though we are now miles apart on that beach. And when I turn back, my ex is *far away looking tiny and hazy* in the distance.

"As I remember my relationship with my ex, it seems like watching reruns of an *old black-and-white television show*. It was compelling the first few times I watched it, but now it feels boring. And I would much rather watch or think about something else ... something fun and new. So I use the remote control and change the channel. I realize there are many colorful shows that interest me. It is time to *enjoy new people and things.*

"From now on, I feel emotionally *detached from my ex*. When I think and remember the relationship we once had, I see it as part of my past and how it made me more mature. It is like looking back on my experience with elementary school. It was appropriate for me then, but I have grown past it and it no longer interests me. It is a part of who I was at one time, but I have long since moved on.

"I am over my ex and it feels good to heal finally and get on with life."

(The Wake-Up)

"I will emerge gently and easily from hypnosis now by counting from one to five. With each number I emerge twenty percent. When I reach the number five, I will return to everyday awareness.

"One . . . emerging twenty percent, beginning to awaken from hypnosis now. (Speak a little louder and stronger.)

"Two . . . forty percent now, as I become fully aware of my body and environment. (Speak louder and stronger.)

"Three . . . sixty percent . . . I look forward to positive results from this hypnosis session. (Speak louder and stronger.)

"Four . . . eighty percent, emerging peaceful and happy. (Strongly assert your intention to emerge.)

"FIVE . . . FIVE . . . FIVE . . . One hundred percent now! Wide awake and fully alert!!!"

Fall Back in Love with Your Mate

*This script will help reignite feelings of
love, tenderness and attraction for your mate.*

"I fall in love again with my mate.

"I remove the calluses of forgetfulness and apathy that have been blocking my loving feelings. Through the power of my mind and with self hypnosis, I *restore my feelings* of intense love, tenderness and attraction for my mate.

"I think now about when I first knew I was in love with my mate. I vividly recall when I obsessively thought about my mate most of the time and how I longed to be with the *most important person in my life*.

(Take a few moments and really remember.)

"When we came together, I loved everything my mate said and did. I embraced all the idiosyncrasies as valued and endearing. We talked for many hours, just the two of us. Even if we ran out of things to say, it was enough *just be together* and bask in each other's presence. Our love went beyond words.

"Over time, we got to know one another and discovered things we had in common and also how we were different. And I was glad of the things that made us different because those things made my mate unique and interesting.

"The idea of being intimate made my heart beat faster and my body tingle with excitement. I remember how appealing and pleasurable it was to touch my mate.

(Take a moment and recall being
intimate the first few times.)

"When we were intimate I felt a deep sense of giving love and being loved. I was able to give and receive pleasure at the same time. I remember how fortunate I felt to share intimacy with my mate.

"As I vividly recall all of the love and passion I felt for my mate, *I fall in love all over again*. Like properly-aged fine wine, the love I feel is now beautifully complex, full of character and nuance. The love I feel reaches a new level.

"I imagine opening a closet door and finding a box of possessions I had forgotten. As I rummage through it, I discover a framed photograph. I cannot see the picture in the frame because the protective glass has become so dirty over time. I wipe away a little of the accumulated grime from the picture frame and the glass, and I recognize my mate's smiling face. I then clean the glass until I realize that I am also in the photograph with my mate. As I look at our body language and expressions in the picture, it is clear that we are still in love with one another. It's good to know that the picture of our *love is still intact* and it is only the frame surrounding it that needs some attention and maintenance. I bring the framed picture out of the closet and place it in a prominent place in my home where I can always see it and take care of it.

(Pause for five seconds.)

"I reclaim the core of love I feel for my mate. I clear away the accumulated debris from my mind and discover that the core of love and passion remains intact. I restore feelings of love for my mate to a prominent place within my mind and heart.

"I think about the next time I will see my mate—as if it was through the eyes of someone deeply in love. I find everything my mate says and does fascinating, charming and lovable.

"I discover that when we get closer, my urge to touch rises from deep within. Those intimate, sexual thoughts and images flash through my mind. My affection for my partner is so strong I want to spend as much time with my mate as possible, whether we are eating, talking, watching television or doing anything else. I am in love and enjoy every minute we are together.

"Every time I see my mate from now on, I will think to myself, 'I'm in love with you.' Each time I do that, the passion and warmth I feel toward my partner increases.

"Falling in love again is glorious! It makes life exciting and worthwhile. I feel alive with love for my mate and find ways to express that love on a daily basis.

"I have fallen in love again."

(The Wake-Up)

"I will emerge gently and easily from hypnosis now by counting from one to five. With each number I emerge twenty percent. When I reach the number five, I will return to everyday awareness.

"One . . . emerging twenty percent, beginning to awaken from hypnosis now. (Speak a little louder and stronger.)

"Two . . . forty percent now, as I become fully aware of my body and environment. (Speak louder and stronger.)

"Three . . . sixty percent . . . I look forward to positive results from this hypnosis session. (Speak louder and stronger.)

"Four . . . eighty percent, emerging peaceful and happy. (Strongly assert your intention to emerge.)

"FIVE . . . FIVE . . . FIVE . . . One hundred percent now! Wide awake and fully alert!!!"

Magnetic Sex Appeal

Boost your expression of natural sex appeal and confidence with this script.

"I exude super sex appeal.

"Through the power of self hypnosis, I program my subconscious mind to accept that *I am a sexually appealing* individual. As this belief expresses itself through self-confidence in my thoughts, words and actions, others will truly be sexually drawn to me. As I now acknowledge my own magnetic sex appeal, other people will believe it too.

"Believe...sex...appeal.

"From now on, I think of myself as a very sexy person. I have an animal magnetism others find irresistible. I think, move and act like a person with magnetic sex appeal. I recognize it as one of my superpowers I use for pleasure and advantage.

"Animal magnetism...sex appeal...superpower.

"Sex appeal is not really about looks. I know this is true because I have seen people who are not very handsome or beautiful, but who are undeniably sexy and magnetic. Sex appeal is an inner awareness of the sexual magnetism that expresses itself through body language, through the voice and through the eyes.

"I now claim that inner awareness of my own amazing sex appeal.

"When I walk into a room, I feel sexy and it is as though my entire being emanates sex appeal that others notice. I walk confidently through any room aware of the effect my magnetic sex appeal has on people.

"There is a look in my eyes of self-assured sex appeal. When others meet my gaze they pick up on my sexy magnetism. Some will be intimidated. Others will be drawn to me. It is like my eyes radiate invisible beams that reach into their minds causing them to notice my *intense sexual energy.*

"Intense...sexual...energy.

"When I talk even about the simplest things, my voice confirms another kind of deep and smoldering sexuality because my sex appeal is supreme. It is a natural part of how I express myself. My sexy voice is part of who I am.

"Natural...sex...appeal.

"I picture a party where friends and strangers are gathered. I walk through the door and think to myself, 'I have magnetic sex appeal.' When I do that, I become conscious of the magnetic force of sex appeal I automatically transmit. I notice some people watch me with great curiosity as I engage others. I speak in relaxed, confident tones. And several new acquaintances are drawn to me and attempt to get my attention.

"I think like a sexually-appealing person. I walk like a sexually attractive person. I talk like a sexually-appealing person.

"Sex appeal is a state of mind. Sex appeal is part of my identity. And like the color of my eyes, having great sex appeal will always be with me."

(The Wake-Up)

"I will emerge gently and easily from hypnosis now by counting from one to five. With each number I emerge twenty percent. When I reach the number five, I will return to everyday awareness.

"One . . . emerging twenty percent, beginning to awaken from hypnosis now. (Speak a little louder and stronger.)

"Two . . . forty percent now, as I become fully aware of my body and environment. (Speak louder and stronger.)

"Three . . . sixty percent . . . I look forward to positive results from this hypnosis session. (Speak louder and stronger.)

"Four . . . eighty percent, emerging peaceful and happy. (Strongly assert your intention to emerge.)

"FIVE . . . FIVE . . . FIVE . . . One hundred percent now! Wide awake and fully alert!!!"

Approach Hot Women

Increase your confidence to approach attractive women with this script.

"I easily and fearlessly approach attractive women.

"Through the power of self hypnosis I now and forever dissolve all my fears about approaching beautiful women. From now on, I feel relaxed and hopeful about respectfully approaching any woman I find appealing.

"Approach…women…relaxed…hopeful.

"In the past I prevented myself from approaching hot women because I imagined they would not be interested in me. I made a baseless assumption that I knew their taste in men and that I would not meet their standard. I now acknowledge that I cannot read the minds of beautiful women. I cannot tell by appearances what kind of a man any beautiful woman prefers.

"I remember that women think differently about what is attractive about the opposite gender. I remember that even the most beautiful women choose to interact with men based on many factors.

"Women…think…differently.

"As I look at a woman I find sexy and attractive, I recognize she has her own ideas about what she finds attractive. She may be drawn to guys with nice faces and physiques, or she may find physical attributes unimportant. A hot woman may appreciate a man who is smart or funny or sweet or shy. She may prefer a man of the world or a down-to-earth guy. A sexy lady may look for a refined, sophisticated man. On the other hand, she might prefer a rugged man with simpler tastes and an easy-going personality.

"The reality is that I cannot know what is on a woman's mind until *I interact with her.* I hereby release any and all assumptions about what a hot woman desires in a guy.

"From now on whenever I see a woman I would like to approach, I take a slow relaxed breath and silently repeat, 'I may be exactly her type,' three times. When I do that, I am filled with courage and respectfully approach her.

"I may be exactly her type.

"I keep in mind that women base their attractions on multiple levels and that I may have the right combination of qualities she finds desirable.

"I picture myself in the drinking area of a nice restaurant. I observe a beautiful woman whom I would like to approach who is sipping a drink. I draw a slow breath and as I release it I silently repeat to myself, 'I may be exactly her type. I may be exactly her type. I may be exactly her ty pe.' The moment I repeat that phrase, I am filled with curiosity to learn more about her. Without hesitation I walk right up to her and make simple conversation.

"As we talk, her body language starts to reveal her interest and receptivity to me. It is clear we have made a connection. At the end of the conversation, I ask her out for a date and give her my number.

"From now on, it is easy for me to approach attractive women. It is no different than approaching less attractive women because each woman has a different taste in men.

"The more beautiful women I approach and interact with, the more likely I am to find out how many hot women find me appealing. I may be just the man they are looking for.

"From now on, I approach beautiful women with ease and confidence."

(The Wake-Up)

"I will emerge gently and easily from hypnosis now by counting from one to five. With each number I emerge twenty percent. When I reach the number five, I will return to everyday awareness.

"One . . . emerging twenty percent, beginning to awaken from hypnosis now. (Speak a little louder and stronger.)

"Two . . . forty percent now, as I become fully aware of my body and environment. (Speak louder and stronger.)

"Three . . . sixty percent . . . I look forward to positive results from this hypnosis session. (Speak louder and stronger.)

"Four . . . eighty percent, emerging peaceful and happy. (Strongly assert your intention to emerge.)

"FIVE . . . FIVE . . . FIVE . . . One hundred percent now! Wide awake and fully alert!!!"

Delay and Intensify Ejaculations

This script will assist the delay of the male climax while it intensifies the experience.

"I want to delay ejaculation until I am ready.

"I now choose to ... delay my ejaculations during sex ... until I give my body permission to climax.

"Delay...intensify...climax.

"As an adult, I enjoy prolonged sexual pleasure. I have as much time to enjoy sex as I want. So, I relax and allow the physical and emotional sensations to wash over me as I experience each activity. When I slow things down ... it becomes easy to *prolong my pleasure* ... and delay orgasm.

"Prolong...pleasure...delay...orgasm.

"I deserve to experience the *most intensely pleasurable orgasms possible.* So I dissolve any and all negative or false ideas ... from the past ... that might have been keeping me ... from taking my time ... and enjoying sex ... for as long as I want it to last. As an adult ... I choose to delay climax ... until the time is *right for me.*

"Enjoy pleasure...delay climax.

"I can let go of memories ... and melt all concerns ... about past experiences ... about sexual performance ... and just concentrate on enjoying myself. Those experiences are far behind me ... faded and distant ... and thanks to self hypnosis ... I realize that things can really be different from now on ... so I can take my time during sex ... and wait as long as I want ... and climax only when I am ready.

"Through the power of posthypnotic suggestion, I can control the sensitivity of my penis during sex. As my penis is touched or rubs against anything during sex, the head automatically feels slightly numb. And as it feels numb, *my penis is less sensitive to friction*, which extends how long I enjoy sexual activity before I climax.

"Less sensitive...extend pleasure.

"When I am ready to climax, I mentally give my body permission to ejaculate ... and I silently say to myself three times in a row, "Maximum pleasure now," ... and when I do, the full sensitivity of my penis returns and I can ejaculate freely and intensely ... because I want to.

"I imagine enjoying sex now. My erection is firm and steady ... and ... it's clear I could delay orgasm for as long as I like ... no matter which sexual acts I experience (take a minute to picture yourself freely engaged in sexual activities you most enjoy).

"Finally, I am ready to experience the height of pleasure. I say silently to myself, 'Maximum pleasure now.' As I do, I observe the mounting pleasure. Again, I think to myself, 'Maximum pleasure now.' It feels like a dam is soon to burst. One last time, I repeat silently, 'Maximum pleasure now!' When I do, I allow myself to ejaculate with powerful total freedom ... reaching new levels of pleasurable fulfillment.

"I have a deep sense of satisfaction that I am able to feel and be sexual and enjoy the fullness of that pleasure from now on. I can delay orgasm for as long as I want to ... until I give myself the mental signal ... and then ... release myself when I am ready ... and intensify my pleasure."

(The Wake-Up)

"I will emerge gently and easily from hypnosis now by counting from one to five. With each number I emerge twenty percent. When I reach the number five, I will return to everyday awareness.

"One . . . emerging twenty percent, beginning to awaken from hypnosis now. (Speak a little louder and stronger.)

"Two . . . forty percent now, as I become fully aware of my body and environment. (Speak louder and stronger.)

"Three . . . sixty percent . . . I look forward to positive results from this hypnosis session. (Speak louder and stronger.)

"Four . . . eighty percent, emerging peaceful and happy. (Strongly assert your intention to emerge.)

"FIVE . . . FIVE . . . FIVE . . . One hundred percent now! Wide awake and fully alert!!!"

Expand Your Comfort Zone

*This script will help motivate you to
broaden your horizons and experience new things.*

"I expand my comfort zone.

"I am ready to go beyond the imaginary boundaries of life I set for myself. I am ready to get moving and explore more of life.

"When a body of water remains still, it becomes stagnant. And stagnant water is dull and lifeless. But water that flows or receives a fresh supply is active and sustains life.

"Staying in a comfort zone encourages stagnation of mind, body and spirit. Expanding my comfort zone will invigorate and refresh my entire being. Doing new things brings to me greater levels of pleasure and satisfaction.

"It is time for me to *experience new things* so I can increase my zest for life. New experiences stir and awaken something deep inside. They stimulate new thoughts and ideas. They help me grow as a person and make life exciting and worth living.

"As I *expand my comfort zone,* things will be unfamiliar to me. I give myself permission to feel new to things … to be a beginner and even to feel awkward sometimes. That is completely natural. If I remember back to when I was a child, new things felt both strange and thrilling at the same time. Those two emotions can complement each other perfectly. Novel experiences expand my awareness and awaken parts of me I never knew existed.

"It is as though I have been living in a vast mansion with dozens of rooms but have limited myself to just a few. But now I am ready to *break through limitations* and open new doors. So I decide to stroll through beautiful but unfamiliar hallways. There are many doors. Some are big and ornate while others are small and modest. I approach a particular door I find unusual and interesting. As I turn the knob and open the door I feel slightly uncomfortable and also excited because I do not know what is beyond the door. I decide I like this feeling because new adventures make me feel more alive.

"Beyond the door a great banquet is taking place with people of different ages, creeds and nationalities. There is a band playing music I have never heard and people dancing in ways I have never witnessed. There are tables lined with exotic foods and a big fountain flowing with sparkling water.

"I cross the threshold of the door so that I can take part in the grand banquet. People smile and engage me in conversation. Someone offers to teach me a new dance. I enjoy myself for a long time and realize that variety is truly the spice of life.

"From this day forward, I seek out new life experiences by doing things I have never done. I learn about subjects of which I know nothing. I go places I have never been. I eat foods I have never tasted. I meet people I have never met.

"If I ever find myself feeling uncomfortable or uncertain about a new situation, I silently repeat to myself, 'It's okay to be uncomfortable outside my comfort zone.' When I do that, I accept my feelings, relax and enjoy myself.

"When this self hypnosis session is over I will embrace situations that encourage me to go beyond my self-imposed limitations. I see life as a great banquet, and that I am a guest of honor.

"I am ready to go forward and expand my comfort zone to feel more alive than ever."

(The Wake-Up)

"I will emerge gently and easily from hypnosis now by counting from one to five. With each number I emerge twenty percent. When I reach the number five, I will return to everyday awareness.

"One . . . emerging twenty percent, beginning to awaken from hypnosis now. (Speak a little louder and stronger.)

"Two . . . forty percent now, as I become fully aware of my body and environment. (Speak louder and stronger.)

"Three . . . sixty percent . . . I look forward to positive results from this hypnosis session. (Speak louder and stronger.)

"Four . . . eighty percent, emerging peaceful and happy. (Strongly assert your intention to emerge.)

"FIVE . . . FIVE . . . FIVE . . . One hundred percent now! Wide awake and fully alert!!!"

Pursue Your Dream

*This script will boost your confidence and
motivate you to pursue your aspirations
in your personal and professional life.*

"I now pursue my dream until it comes true.

"There is something I want to do, be or have more than anything else in the world. I think about what it is right now. It is something I have yet to manifest in my life. With the full support and resources of my subconscious mind, I choose to do everything in my power to pursue that dream until it is accomplished!

"There may be people in my life who tell me my dream is impossible. They say such things perhaps because they never achieved their biggest goal. Maybe they did not try hard enough. Maybe they gave up too soon. They speak from the pain of their own failures. Therefore, I choose to disregard their words.

"Instead, I observe examples of those who have accomplished a similar dream to mine. They are like teachers and guides who educate and inspire me.

"Like those who have already succeeded, I possess the courage, determination and fortitude to follow my dream and see it through to completion. Any negative words and attitudes of others only strengthen my resolve. They remind me how much I believe in myself and that I will get what I set my mind to achieve.

"Anything worth achieving requires effort. I hereby remove the shackles of apathy and lethargy from around my ankles that slowed me down. I look forward to doing the work required to fulfill my dream with tireless enthusiasm.

"If I require information, I research it. If I need to network with people who can help me, I seek them out. If I require assistance from institutions, I contact them. If there are skills I must acquire, I learn them. If there are activities I must perform, I perform them.

"I now imagine what my dream is going to be like when it has become reality. I picture what it looks like, sounds like and any other sensations that accompany it.

(Spend a full 30 seconds imagining this.)

"I think about the joy and bliss I will experience when my dream has come true. I look back at the time and dedication required to accomplish it. I realize it was all worthwhile. Not only did I get exactly what I wanted, but I have proven that I am capable of doing amazing things. I feel as though I can accomplish anything I desire from now on.

"I accept that some things in life take time to accomplish, and that there may be obstacles. If I encounter a delay or setback I repeat to myself, 'I overcome all setbacks.' As I do, my resolve to succeed becomes even stronger and I search for ways to surmount the obstacle.

"Every individual step on this journey takes me closer to the fulfillment of my dream. After this self hypnosis session, I will recognize *the very next step* needed to get closer to getting what I want. Once I have determined it, I immediately *get moving* and initiate that important step. I *take action* because action leads to results.

"I follow my bliss. I go for my dream."

(The Wake-Up)

"I will emerge gently and easily from hypnosis now by counting from one to five. With each number I emerge twenty

percent. When I reach the number five, I will return to everyday awareness.

"One . . . emerging twenty percent, beginning to awaken from hypnosis now. (Speak a little louder and stronger.)

"Two . . . forty percent now, as I become fully aware of my body and environment. (Speak louder and stronger.)

"Three . . . sixty percent . . . I look forward to positive results from this hypnosis session. (Speak louder and stronger.)

"Four . . . eighty percent, emerging peaceful and happy. (Strongly assert your intention to emerge.)

"FIVE . . . FIVE . . . FIVE . . . One hundred percent now! Wide awake and fully alert!!!"

Stop Overreacting

Control and prevent exaggerated emotional reactions to life with this script.

"I stop overreacting to events and circumstances.

"In the past there were times when how I dealt with disagreeable people or situations was inappropriate and immature. Those outbursts of emotion were out of line, and led to unfortunate actions and embarrassment.

"From now on I take control of my emotions and stop overreacting. I use self hypnosis to regulate my expressions of emotion when confronted with any disagreeable person or situation.

"It's as though there is a child within who represents the emotional part of me and I am its parent. We have a marvelous relationship. I enjoy observing the child express joy, frustration, sorrow, gratitude and a full range of human emotions. It is wonderful to feel and express healthy feelings. A range of healthy emotions make life dynamic and interesting.

"However, the child within sometimes behaves immaturely and needs reassurance and guidance. I know when the childlike part of me feels upset and I can sense when any emotions are inappropriate to the situation. Whenever I sense those inappropriate emotions, I calm my inner child by drawing and releasing a slow deep breath and repeating, 'Take it easy. Everything is okay.' When I do, that child within feels safe and any negative emotions come easily under my control.

"I imagine being in a restaurant and a beverage has spilled all over my clothes. I can sense the child within me feeling embarrassed and upset and that turbulent feelings are about to erupt. Just then, I take a slow deep breath and let it out calmly and slowly. I silently say to the child within, 'Take it easy. Everything is okay.' As I do that, I recognize that it's just a spilt drink. It is no big deal. Sometimes in life, people spill things. It is actually rather funny--so I chuckle at what has happened. I am able to laugh at myself and at the situation.

"With every passing day, the child within me learns and grows through experience and my guidance. I gain greater control over all of my emotional reactions. I relax and take things in stride. I am able to handle people and situations with dignity and grace. I see now that small disturbances are a natural part of life while I can choose to remain calm as I deal with them.

"I now picture myself on a plane with many passengers. While most of the flight is smooth, the plane suddenly hits some mild turbulence. I recognize the situation is normal and is no big deal. However, the passenger next to me is new to flying and shows signs of great distress. To relax my fellow passenger, I comment that turbulence is a natural part of flying and everything is okay. When I do that, the passenger immediately smiles and calms down and feels much better.

"In a similar way, I know that when minor things seem to go wrong it's a normal part of the journey of life. If I feel signs of distress, I can immediately remind myself that everything is okay. And when I do, I immediately draw a slow breath and compose myself.

"It feels good to respond calmly and appropriately to people and circumstances that used to upset me. Now I know I can handle myself in all situations with strength, dignity and maturity.

"With every passing day I gain more and more control over my emotional reactions. Exercising self control makes me feel good."

(The Wake-Up)

"I will emerge gently and easily from hypnosis now by counting from one to five. With each number I emerge twenty percent. When I reach the number five, I will return to everyday awareness.

"One . . . emerging twenty percent, beginning to awaken from hypnosis now. (Speak a little louder and stronger.)

"Two . . . forty percent now, as I become fully aware of my body and environment. (Speak louder and stronger.)

"Three . . . sixty percent . . . I look forward to positive results from this hypnosis session. (Speak louder and stronger.)

"Four . . . eighty percent, emerging peaceful and happy. (Strongly assert your intention to emerge.)

"FIVE . . . FIVE . . . FIVE . . . One hundred percent now! Wide awake and fully alert!!!"

Stop Cussing

*With this script you can quit using curse words
and foul language during conversation.*

"I choose to stop cussing.

"I acknowledge that using foul language is an inappropriate way of expressing myself. Cursing and off-color language create pictures in the mind which sometimes embarrass and offend people.

"Cussing has no place in my life.

"From now on I present myself in a dignified manner through my choice of words. I decide to express myself to family, friends, associates and strangers only using language that reveals *the respect I feel* for myself and for others.

"I *stop cussing.*

"I now take full responsibility for the words I speak. Moreover, with the help of self hypnosis, I *entirely eliminate cusswords* from my vocabulary.

"I abolish cusswords and all foul language from my speech patterns now and forever.

"There may have been a time when I believed using cusswords would make me appear strong and mature. Cussing may have been a way I attempted to fit in with my peers. Now that I am more mature, I realize cussing is a sign of immaturity and limited thinking.

"I picture a big blackboard in front of me. Written in gray chalk are all of the cusswords I have used. Next to each cussword is a drawing of the image the cussword brings to mind. The handwriting is mine, but it looks very childish—the way I might have written things when I was eight years old.

And the drawings are very crude, the way an adolescent might draw vulgar graffiti. The words and images are inappropriate for dignified adults.

"So I take a big eraser and wipe away each and every cussword. As each word is erased from the blackboard, it is removed from my vocabulary. Chalk dust fills the air and I realize how polluted my language had been. As the dust dissipates, I am glad to remove that negative language. The blackboard is now clear so I can express myself positive, cleanly and clearly.

"In large letters I write the words, 'DIGNITY AND RESPECT.' These words remind me to use only language that reflects dignity and shows respect for the person I am speaking to.

"Now that cusswords have been replaced by dignity and respect, I feel as though those ugly words are non-existent for me. When I hear them from other people, they sound odd and ridiculous.

"If I think or say a cussword, I repeat to myself: 'Dignity and respect.' Then I realize how silly the cussword is and I erase it from the blackboard in my mind.

"From this time forward, it is easy for me to stop cussing and to find other ways to express my thoughts and feelings more accurately."

(The Wake-Up)

"I will emerge gently and easily from hypnosis now by counting from one to five. With each number I emerge twenty percent. When I reach the number five, I will return to everyday awareness.

"One . . . emerging twenty percent, beginning to awaken from hypnosis now. (Speak a little louder and stronger.)

"Two . . . forty percent now, as I become fully aware of my body and environment. (Speak louder and stronger.)

"Three . . . sixty percent . . . I look forward to positive results from this hypnosis session. (Speak louder and stronger.)

"Four . . . eighty percent, emerging peaceful and happy. (Strongly assert your intention to emerge.)

"FIVE . . . FIVE . . . FIVE . . . One hundred percent now! Wide awake and fully alert!!!"

More Loving and Affectionate

*Speak and behave with more love and affection
toward your family and friends.*

"Day by day, I express more love and affection.

"I embrace the display of affection to those I care about in my life. As I become more openly loving I make stronger emotional connections that improve the quality of my relationships and my life.

"Perhaps when I was young, my family didn't openly express love and affection enough. Or, maybe I wasn't very affectionate. Nevertheless, as I have matured I have come to recognize the importance and long lasting value of showing love and affection to those around me.

"It's time to create bonds of intimacy by freely saying and demonstrating how much I love and appreciate the intimate people in my life. So I find opportunities to communicate to others how much I care about them. I choose to speak in loving words ... to show physical affection ... and to reveal love through my actions.

"From now on, being loving and affectionate comes to me naturally and easily. I discover that when I express love and affection more freely, I automatically feel happy and more relaxed. Feelings of love and warmth have a healing, soothing, uplifting effect on my body as well as on my mind. So being loving and affectionate not only feels good, it is also healthy.

"I imagine a bright golden yellow sphere of light, like a miniature sun, in the center of my chest. It radiates a warm, powerful force of love and tenderness throughout every fiber of my being. I imagine I am drenched in the golden warmth of love that extends out from me in every direction. I am now filled with feelings of love and a strong desire to express loving affection to others. I realize that expressing love and affection are part of my true nature.

"I think of myself as a loving and affectionate person. As I allow love and affection to flow from me freely, my life is greatly enriched in so many ways. The more I show love and affection, the more love, appreciation and affection I am able to receive.

"Every chance I get, I express love and affection toward those I care about. And when I do, I feel good about myself and my connections with others.

"The warmth of love fills my life, and sharing it becomes an important part of my everyday experience."

(The Wake-Up)

"I will emerge gently and easily from hypnosis now by counting from one to five. With each number I emerge twenty percent. When I reach the number five, I will return to everyday awareness.

"One . . . emerging twenty percent, beginning to awaken from hypnosis now. (Speak a little louder and stronger.)

"Two . . . forty percent now, as I become fully aware of my body and environment. (Speak louder and stronger.)

"Three . . . sixty percent . . . I look forward to positive results from this hypnosis session. (Speak louder and stronger.)

"Four . . . eighty percent, emerging peaceful and happy. (Strongly assert your intention to emerge.)

"FIVE . . . FIVE . . . FIVE . . . One hundred percent now! Wide awake and fully alert!!!"

Embrace Your Age

*Accept your age and enjoy your
maturity with this script.*

"I embrace myself at my current age.

"I enjoy and *appreciate my current age* and recognize it as perfectly suited to me. I dissolve and release all conflicting, negative and discouraging thoughts and feelings about my age. Through the power of self hypnosis I *reframe my thoughts and feelings about my age* so that I may be *perfectly happy and confident* at this time of my life.

"I am proud of my age.

"I choose to *see the beauty and merits of every age group* and every phase of life. I view myself as attractive and interesting at my current age. Time brings experience. Every year I become wiser and my character deepens. I know and understand things that were impossible to recognize when I was younger.

"I utterly reject the distorted and limited perspective of age as presented through the media and popular culture. I now expand my view to recognize that *every age is appealing and relevant*, including and especially my current age.

"I never again lie about my age or refer to my age in a negative or derogatory way. If I ever notice myself making an unkind remark about my age, I immediately say, 'I love being this age!' When I do that, any negative feelings are obliterated and replaced with feelings of pride, dignity and confidence.

"Beauty and handsomeness apply to every age and phase of life. My face and body at this phase are natural, attractive and have their own appealing qualities. My mind thinks as an adult and my activities are perfectly suited for this period of my life. I look, think and act exactly as I should at this age.

"I imagine celebrating my birthday and I'm looking at a birthday cake with lighted candles in the shape of numerals that display my current age. I look at the number with great pride, happiness and confidence. As I blow out the candles I make a wish to *experience all the joy that this age has to offer*. I determine to get the most out of each and every day and to feel absolutely comfortable with myself, inside and out.

"As I embrace my current age and see it as wonderful and precious, it means I simultaneously embrace myself in a similar way. The more I love and accept myself in every way possible, the more joy and gratitude I feel to be alive.

"When I emerge from this self hypnosis session in just a few moments, I choose to have a renewed sense of purpose and satisfaction about my life.

"And I celebrate and love my age from this time forward."

(The Wake-Up)

"I will emerge gently and easily from hypnosis now by counting from one to five. With each number I emerge twenty percent. When I reach the number five, I will return to everyday awareness.

"One . . . emerging twenty percent, beginning to awaken from hypnosis now. (Speak a little louder and stronger.)

"Two . . . forty percent now, as I become fully aware of my body and environment. (Speak louder and stronger.)

"Three . . . sixty percent . . . I look forward to positive results from this hypnosis session. (Speak louder and stronger.)

"Four . . . eighty percent, emerging peaceful and happy. (Strongly assert your intention to emerge.)

"FIVE . . . FIVE . . . FIVE . . . One hundred percent now! Wide awake and fully alert!!!"

Love My Body As It Is

Appreciate your body as it is with this script.

"I love my body exactly as it is.

"The human body comes in many colors, shapes and sizes. We are all different and meant to be that way. I, therefore, affirm my unique body as attractive and just right as it is.

"My body is attractive and just right.

"I utterly reject the extreme and limited body ideals presented through the media and popular culture. I now expand my view of what an attractive body looks like to include my own body.

"My body is beautiful just the way it is!

"I will never again refer to my body or any part of my body in a negative way. If I ever make a negative remark about my body, I immediately tell myself: 'My body looks just as it is!'

"I choose to treasure the shape, size and appearance of my body in its current condition from this moment forward. I dissolve and replace all disempowering attitudes about my body with healthy, positive thoughts. Embracing and loving my body sends an encouraging message to my body to feel healthy and happy.

"I imagine looking at my body in a three way mirror, one that shows all the angles. I wholeheartedly accept and love each part of my body. I love my head, my ears, eyes, nose and mouth. I have a unique and good-looking face.

"I love my neck and shape of my shoulders. My chest and back are shapely and appealing. My arms, hands and fingers are ideally formed. I appreciate my natural stomach and the pleasing curves of my buttocks. My genitals are attractive and sexy. My legs are the perfect length and my feet and toes are nicely proportioned.

"The ways my face and body come together are just right!

"As I frequently express love and appreciation for my body the *greater happiness and confidence* I experience each day. Every time I look in the mirror when I am alone, I say to myself: 'You look good.' And then, with a warm smile, I feel the appreciation flow on from my body to mind.

"It feels so good to totally accept the way I look today. I realize now that I am blessed to have such a nice body and face. I celebrate my body, and from this time forward I consider it attractive and appealing the way it is."

(The Wake-Up)

"I will emerge gently and easily from hypnosis now by counting from one to five. With each number I emerge twenty percent. When I reach the number five, I will return to everyday awareness.

"One . . . emerging twenty percent, beginning to awaken from hypnosis now. (Speak a little louder and stronger.)

"Two . . . forty percent now, as I become fully aware of my body and environment. (Speak louder and stronger.)

"Three . . . sixty percent . . . I look forward to positive results from this hypnosis session. (Speak louder and stronger.)

"Four . . . eighty percent, emerging peaceful and happy. (Strongly assert your intention to emerge.)

"FIVE . . . FIVE . . . FIVE . . . One hundred percent now! Wide awake and fully alert!!!"

Shrink Cancerous Tumors

Use this script with your licensed medical care provider to assist in the reduction and elimination of tumors. Enhance the mind-body connection!

"I call upon every power available to me to *shrink cancerous tumors* and restore my optimum health.

"*Shrink tumors.* Restore health.

"I now utilize all of my physical and mental resources to eradicate cancerous cells from my body and return to optimum health.

"*Resources. Eradicate cancer. Optimum health.*

"I am like a confident and determined Ruler who makes wise decisions to defend my realm. I command my specialized army of warriors to kill any and all cancerous invaders. I command my fighters to kill every cell in the tumor. I command my fighters to banish cancer from that realm of my body forever.

"*Fight. Kill. Invaders.*

(Pause five seconds.)

"I imagine it is a sunny day, and I am holding a magnifying glass over an ice cube. Using the magnifier, I point and focus a narrow, intense light beam on the ice cube. I watch as it begins to melt. It drips and shrinks…shrinks…smaller and smaller. Finally, the watery remains evaporate to nothing. I melt all remaining ice cubes using the same magnified focus until no ice cubes remain.

"The ice cubes are like tumors and as I focus my intention to dissolve them, it's like I am focusing the powerful rays of the sun to melt ice cubes of cancerous tumors. And the tumors dissolve until there are only healthy cells.

"As I do that, I also melt and release any hurts, shocks or remorse my mind may have harbored ... consciously or unconsciously. I release the hurts from the past and turn my attention to this new day. It is time to let go of any deep hurts, resentments or hidden grief that may have been gnawing away at me. I forgive and release all of the past because it has gone now. I choose to fill my present reality with life, joy and vitality. I approve of myself.

"And as I take my next slow deep breath, I affirm all of life and I harmonize with my body and with the physical world."

(Draw a breath and release it, and
allow joyful feelings.)

"I declare that all things work together for my healing and for my highest good. I recognize that all circumstances may be used as opportunities to learn and grow as a human being.

"As I undergo medical procedures to help eradicate cancerous tumors, I become very relaxed and take slow deep breaths. When I do that, I become very peaceful and positive about the effectiveness of the medical intervention. As I affirm my own strength and ability in the healing process, I recover quickly from all medical procedures.

"Peaceful... therapy... recover.

(Pause five seconds.)

"I imagine a day in the near future. Any and all cancerous tumors have been vanquished, and I am cancer-free!

"Not only am I relieved that my tumors are now gone, I also feel a sense of empowerment that I helped make that possible. This experience has given me greater strength and self-esteem!.

"Cancer-free. Tumors gone.

"This experience is my opportunity to live life more fully. That is something I begin to do right now.

"Live Fully Now."

(The Wake-Up)

"I will emerge gently and easily from hypnosis now by counting from one to five. With each number I emerge twenty percent. When I reach the number five, I will return to everyday awareness.

"One . . . emerging twenty percent, beginning to awaken from hypnosis now. (Speak a little louder and stronger.)

"Two . . . forty percent now, as I become fully aware of my body and environment. (Speak louder and stronger.)

"Three . . . sixty percent . . . I look forward to positive results from this hypnosis session. (Speak louder and stronger.)

"Four . . . eighty percent, emerging peaceful and happy. (Strongly assert your intention to emerge.)

"FIVE . . . FIVE . . . FIVE . . . One hundred percent now! Wide awake and fully alert!!!"

Fibromyalgia Relief

*Relieve or reduce the symptoms associated
with fibromyalgia with this script.*

"I experience relief from fibromyalgia.

"I acknowledge that the subconscious mind is very powerful, and it runs billions of functions and processes of my body at every moment. I also recognize that self hypnosis may be used to alter body conditions and sensations.

"My body functions and processes are under the control of my subconscious mind. And self hypnosis allows me to communicate with that part of my mind.

"Whatever the cause of fibromyalgia may be, I direct my subconscious to *discontinue all MY symptoms* so I may enjoy a healthy body, free of discomfort.

"All muscle pain stops. All muscle spasms stop. My energy returns to normal. I sleep easily and deeply throughout the night. Any and all other symptoms of fibromyalgia completely discontinue.

"As I take the time now to learn *to relax* with the help of self hypnosis, I can experience immediate relief from *all symptoms of fibromyalgia.*

"I imagine myself wrapped in a deep blue blanket of relaxation and healing. I picture the blanket wrapped around my entire body, from my head to my toes so only my face is showing.

(Take 15 seconds and fully imagine it.)

"I feel safe and secure covered in the soft, cozy blanket. I feel like a baby who is nurtured by a strong and protective guardian. Like a happy and well-loved infant, I feel utterly peaceful and completely worry-free now. All sense of the past or future disappears and is replaced by utter comfort in the here and now.

"And now I picture the deep blue color as liquid light that not only surrounds me, but also fills every part of my being here and now.

(Take 15 seconds to imagine
the blue light filling you.)

"My breathing becomes more relaxed and regular now. My heartbeat slows down to a safe and comfortable rhythm.

"The muscles of my entire body, including my scalp, my temples and my jaw loosen and relax. Loosen and relax. The nerve endings of every part of me calm down and relax. Calm down and relax. My thoughts are gentle and quiet. My feelings are purely blissful and deeply tranquil.

"Now I imagine I am immersed in a soothing warm bath and that in this moment everything is fine and working beautifully in my body, my mind and in the very deep places of my being. In this timeless moment, all is well. I am safe. I am supported. I am at peace with myself. I am at peace with the world. I can relax. I can let go here and now. Here and now.

(Take a full 30 seconds to
experience calm.)

"After I emerge from this self hypnosis session, I will continue to feel safe, supported and peaceful. Any and all symptoms of fibromyalgia fade utterly into nothingness. And what remains is a relaxed and healthy state of body and mind.

"I look forward to a healthy body and peaceful mind as my way of being every day.

"If I ever notice any of the old symptoms recurring, I draw three slow relaxing breaths and silently repeat, 'My body and feelings are calm and healthy. All is well.' When I do this, those symptoms immediately disappear and I will feel comfortable and clear-headed."

(The Wake-Up)

"I will emerge gently and easily from hypnosis now by counting from one to five. With each number I emerge twenty percent. When I reach the number five, I will return to everyday awareness.

"One . . . emerging twenty percent, beginning to awaken from hypnosis now. (Speak a little louder and stronger.)

"Two . . . forty percent now, as I become fully aware of my body and environment. (Speak louder and stronger.)

"Three . . . sixty percent . . . I look forward to positive results from this hypnosis session. (Speak louder and stronger.)

"Four . . . eighty percent, emerging peaceful and happy. (Strongly assert your intention to emerge.)

"FIVE . . . FIVE . . . FIVE . . . One hundred percent now! Wide awake and fully alert!!!"

Tinnitus Relief

End the ringing in your ears—
or reduce it—with this script.

"The ringing in my ears now goes away.

"My body functions and processes are under the control of my unconscious mind. And self hypnosis allows me to communicate with that part of my mind. Whatever the cause of my ears ringing, I direct my unconscious mind to *discontinue the ringing* immediately.

"Discontinue...ringing...immediately.

"Sometimes the source of tinnitus can be psychological. Regardless of the cause, the ringing of the ears must stop and my subconscious will not replace it with any other discomfort or unpleasant conditions of the body.

"Stop...ringing.

"Tinnitus can sometimes be stress-related. As I take the time now to loosen the muscles of my body, particularly in my face and jaw, and that stress is relieved, I may experience complete relief from tinnitus.

"Tinnitus...relief...complete.

"I imagine myself wrapped in a deep blue blanket of healing relaxation. I picture it around my entire body, from my head to my toes so that just my face is showing.

(Take 15 seconds and fully imagine it.)

"I feel safe and secure covered in the soft, cozy blanket. I feel like a baby who is nurtured by a strong and protective guardian. Like a happy and well-loved baby, I feel utterly peaceful and completely worry-free now. All negative emotions dissolve entirely and are replaced by utter comfort in the here and now.

"And now I picture someone pouring a deep blue light right down through the top of my head. A tranquil sensation fills my brain and reaches every corner of my middle ear.

(Take 15 seconds to imagine the blue light filling you.)

"My breathing becomes more relaxed and regular now. My heartbeat slows to a safe and comfortable rhythm.

"The muscles of my entire body—including my scalp, my temples and my jaw—loosen and relax. Loosen and relax. The nerve endings of every part of me calm down and relax. Calm down and relax. My thoughts are gentle and quiet ones. My feelings are purely blissful and I experience deep serenity.

"And now I imagine I am immersed in a soothing warm bath and that in this moment everything is fine and working beautifully in my body, in my mind and in the very deep places of my being. In this timeless moment, all is well. I am safe. I am supported. I am at peace with myself. I am at peace with the world. I can relax. I can let go here and now. Here and now.

(Take a full 30 seconds to experience calm.)

"With the stress gone I may discover the absence of ringing in my ears now ... or in a few minutes. Instead, I hear only the sound of my own voice and noises in my environment.

"Ringing...gone...now.

"If I ever again notice a ringing in my ears, I take three slow relaxing breaths and silently repeat: 'All is well. I am at peace.' When I do that, the ringing disappears and my hearing returns to normal.

"Ringing…disappears.

"I imagine after this session is over what it is like to eliminate tinnitus from my life. It feels so good to hear normally again. I imagine that the relief continues throughout the rest of the day and every day thereafter. After a week, the experience of tinnitus will seem a distant memory.

"I am forever free of tinnitus."

(The Wake-Up)

"I will emerge gently and easily from hypnosis now by counting from one to five. With each number I emerge twenty percent. When I reach the number five, I will return to everyday awareness.

"One . . . emerging twenty percent, beginning to awaken from hypnosis now. (Speak a little louder and stronger.)

"Two . . . forty percent now, as I become fully aware of my body and environment. (Speak louder and stronger.)

"Three . . . sixty percent . . . I look forward to positive results from this hypnosis session. (Speak louder and stronger.)

"Four . . . eighty percent, emerging peaceful and happy. (Strongly assert your intention to emerge.)

"FIVE . . . FIVE . . . FIVE . . . One hundred percent now! Wide awake and fully alert!!!"

Freedom from Eczema

Eczema symptoms can be
relieved or reduced with this script.

"I experience complete freedom from eczema.

"My bodily functions and processes are under the control of my subconscious mind. Self hypnosis allows me to communicate with that part of my mind. Whatever the cause of eczema, I hereby direct my subconscious mind to use all of its amazing resources to heal my skin and eliminate eczema once and for all.

"Heal...skin...eliminate...eczema.

"After this self hypnosis session, skin affected by eczema begins to heal. All rashes, patches, bumps, itching, dry or sore skin diminish hour by hour, day by day—until all that remains is my clear and healthy skin.

"I picture clear, healthy skin.

"The source of eczema is sometimes psychosomatic. Regardless of the cause, I now instruct my mind to end this eczema condition. The skin eruptions must stop and my subconscious will not replace them with any other uncomfortable, embarrassing body conditions.

"Stop...eruptions...stop.

"Eczema is sometimes associated with stress. I consider the sources of stress in my life and eliminate them wherever possible. As I frequently apply self hypnosis to further eliminate this condition from my body, I may experience complete freedom from eczema.

"I imagine myself wrapped in a soothing blue blanket of relaxation and tranquility. I picture it around my entire body, from my head to my toes so just my face is showing.

(Take 15 seconds and fully imagine it.)

"I feel safe and secure covered in the soft, cozy blue blanket. I feel like a baby who is being taken care of by a strong and protective guardian. Like a happy and well-loved infant, I feel utterly peaceful and completely worry-free now. All negative emotions dissolve entirely, replaced by utter comfort here and now.

"My breathing becomes more relaxed and regular now. My heartbeat slows down to a safe and comfortable rhythm.

"The muscles of my entire body loosen and relax. Loosen and relax. The nerve endings of every part of me calm down and relax. Calm down and relax. My thoughts are gentle and quiet ones. My feelings are blissfully pure with a deep serenity.

(Take a full 30 seconds to experience calm.)

"And now I imagine I am immersed in a warm bath of deep blue liquid light. Every part of my skin is soothed, warmed and healed by this light bath. I picture any patches of eczema fading ... fading ... until all that is left is clear, comfortable, beautiful skin. It is a glorious experience!

(Take 15 seconds to imagine clear and
healthy skin and feel glad.)

"With the stress gone I may discover freedom from any itching, soreness or any other unpleasant sensations now ... or in a few minutes. The process of healing has begun so I begin to notice improvement in the look and sensations of my skin.

"Skin. Healing. Now.

"If I ever again notice any symptoms of eczema I take three slow relaxing breaths and silently repeat, 'All is well. I am at peace.' When I do that, the healing power of my subconscious is reactivated to return my skin to a condition of perfect health.

"Perfect...skin...healing.

"I picture myself in a couple of days examining my skin and feeling delighted to notice tremendous improvement in its color and condition. I know that everyday my skin is clearing. And, that I am free from eczema from this time forward."

(The Wake-Up)

"I will emerge gently and easily from hypnosis now by counting from one to five. With each number I emerge twenty percent. When I reach the number five, I will return to everyday awareness.

"One . . . emerging twenty percent, beginning to awaken from hypnosis now. (Speak a little louder and stronger.)

"Two . . . forty percent now, as I become fully aware of my body and environment. (Speak louder and stronger.)

"Three . . . sixty percent . . . I look forward to positive results from this hypnosis session. (Speak louder and stronger.)

"Four . . . eighty percent, emerging peaceful and happy. (Strongly assert your intention to emerge.)

"FIVE . . . FIVE . . . FIVE . . . One hundred percent now! Wide awake and fully alert!!!"

IBS Relief

*Irritable Bowel Syndrome can be
reduced or relieved with this script.*

"I experience relief from the symptoms of irritable bowel syndrome.

"My subconscious is very powerful and runs billions of functions and processes of my body at every moment. Moreover, I recognize that hypnosis may be used to alter many body conditions and sensations.

"My bodily functions and processes are under the control of my unconscious mind. Self hypnosis allows me to communicate with that part of my mind. Whatever the source of IBS, I direct my subconscious to eliminate the symptoms and help heal the cause so that I may enjoy a healthy body, free of all discomfort.

"I recognize the symptoms of IBS can relate to a person's prolonged stress levels. Stress is my body's fight or flight mechanism. Whenever it is activated, it protects me by temporarily shutting down my digestive system so I can escape danger. When the danger subsides, the stress mechanism is deactivated and my digestive functions *return to normal.*

"Because of busy modern life, I may have forgotten to *deactivate the stress mechanism.* But through self hypnosis, I now switch off the fight or flight response, and switch on my healthy digestive system.

"I imagine I stand in a futuristic control room of my own body. There is a computer that displays a hologram of my body and monitors its stress level. The entire hologram blinks bright red, indicating a high level of stress. I draw a deep breath and as I exhale I say the words, 'Deactivate stress now.'

(Draw a deep breath, exhale and
say: 'deactivate stress now.')

"When I do that, the hologram stops blinking red. It turns into a relaxing blue color, indicating a calm, sustainable level. As I look at the readout for my stomach, digestive tract and bowels, I see that the oxygenation have been restored to normal, relaxed function levels. And I instantly feel much better.

"I now pretend I am wrapped in a deep blue blanket of healing relaxation and tranquility.

(Take 15 seconds and fully imagine it.)

""I feel safe and secure covered in the soft, cozy blanket. I now feel utterly peaceful and worry-free. From this place of comfort, I can let go of the past and look forward to the new me.

"My breathing is slow and rhythmic.

(Take three slow, rhythmic breaths)

"I can breathe better and bring in fresh air to every part of my body. With each exhalation, I release all that I no longer need . . . so that I can take in the new.

(Take a few slow and
easy breaths with that in mind.)

"If I ever feel any symptoms of IBS, I think of myself covered in the blue blanket of relaxation. I draw three, slow rhythmic breaths and repeat silently to myself, 'I am safe and secure. All is well.' When I do that, any undesirable symptoms quickly dissolve and perfect balance and harmony are restored.

"As I take the time to learn to relax and shut off the stress mechanism, I experience immediate and lasting relief from the symptoms of IBS."

(The Wake-Up)

"I will emerge gently and easily from hypnosis now by counting from one to five. With each number I emerge twenty percent. When I reach the number five, I will return to everyday awareness.

"One . . . emerging twenty percent, beginning to awaken from hypnosis now. (Speak a little louder and stronger.)

"Two . . . forty percent now, as I become fully aware of my body and environment. (Speak louder and stronger.)

"Three . . . sixty percent . . . I look forward to positive results from this hypnosis session. (Speak louder and stronger.)

"Four . . . eighty percent, emerging peaceful and happy. (Strongly assert your intention to emerge.)

"FIVE . . . FIVE . . . FIVE . . . One hundred percent now! Wide awake and fully alert!!!"

Feel Fine with Heights

Eliminate your fear of high places with this script.

"I overcome fear of heights.

"Through the power of self hypnosis I am able to reprogram my mind and body to feel comfortable with high places. It doesn't matter when or why the trouble began. What matters is that I choose to feel *and think differently about heights* from now on, and this session empowers me to do that.

"By the time I have completed this self hypnosis session, I will feel much more relaxed about heights. Any worries will have diminished tremendously and will continue to do so until they are completely gone and forgotten. And all that will be left is a normal healthy response to high places.

"Having a healthy respect for heights is a natural and good thing. It's hard-wired in human beings to protect us and *there's nothing wrong* with that. So I can *feel comfortable* knowing that *my mind protects me* from potential danger.

"But for some people, that healthy respect for high places goes too far and tricks the mind and body into feeling drawn to the edge and like they can't move forward or back. This is like a mouse that freezes in place when it thinks a cat is nearby. That is a wise response if there is a real cat. But when there is *no significant danger*, there is no need for the mouse to feel that way. It can *relax and keep moving* while it looks out for the real cat. In the meantime, it is reasonably safe.

"In the same way, I have been afraid of a danger that is not real because even while in high places I am reasonably safe. There are usually safeguards in place to keep me secure. However, somewhere along the way, I imagined a threat to my well-being and that triggered an unpleasant response to heights.

"The good news is that I can use my imagination now with self hypnosis to have a relaxed response to high places. Since my imagination got me into this trouble with how I deal with heights, I can use my imagination to get me out of it.

"Right now I am going to think about a high place where I felt the worst, because I'm going to change my response.

(Think about when you were in a high place that made you uncomfortable. Allow yourself to feel the discomfort. Spend 30 seconds to do this.)

"As I think about that high place, I feel fearful and I may notice tension in my body. That is okay because I'm going to alter the way my mind responds. I am going to remove all emotion from that experience so my subconscious starts to feel differently about that memory and all other memories like it.

"When my subconscious feels calm and relaxed about those memories, I will feel comfortable too, and I'll forget all about the problems I had with high places.

"To do that, I think about a relaxing place I have visited to get away from everything. It might be the beach or the forest or anywhere I remember where I felt the *freedom to relax.*

(Think about a specific place where you have felt super relaxed.)

"I remember the relaxing place like I'm there now. I will know I have done this correctly when I start truly feeling at peace in my mind and body.

(Take ten seconds to recall it fully.)

"As calm, relaxed and good as I feel, I'm going to count backwards from three to one. And with each number I use my imagination to double the good feelings ... to feel twice as calm and comfortable with each number.

"Three ... I feel twice as relaxed and comfortable. Two ... doubling the calm and peaceful sensations. One... I imagine feeling as happy and relaxed as ever.

"I feel so utterly tranquil and good that it's impossible to imagine feeling any other way now.

"Now I pretend I am sitting near a television. The television screen is a bit far from me and I am watching an outdated video of one of those high places from the past. As I watch from a distance, I continue to feel calm and comfortable.

"I pretend I am using a remote control and fast forwarding to other old videos of high places I've seen before. There might be high stairs, long escalators, or storied balconies involved; but now I feel calm and comfortable. In fact, I feel disinterested in these old videos because they have no
value to me.

"I am a little surprised by my lack of reaction to high places on the television screen. As I fast forward through every high place I've ever visited, I have the same disinterest.

"So I just shrug my shoulders now and say, 'I feel calm as I move forward.'

"I let the television screen fade from my thoughts, and think once more of the high place where I used to feel the worst. But I discover that I continue to feel calm and comfortable. I may even forget that it ever bothered me in the first place.

"And from now on, this is the way I will think and feel about all high places I encounter each day. As I approach them I will repeat to myself, 'I feel calm as I move forward.' When I do that, I remain calm and indifferent to the high place. I can choose to forget all about those old worn out memories because they no longer affect me.

"From this time forward, I feel fine about high places, because my response to them has changed."

(The Wake-Up)

"I will emerge gently and easily from hypnosis now by counting from one to five. With each number I emerge twenty percent. When I reach the number five, I will return to everyday awareness.

"One . . . emerging twenty percent, beginning to awaken from hypnosis now. (Speak a little louder and stronger.)

"Two . . . forty percent now, as I become fully aware of my body and environment. (Speak louder and stronger.)

"Three . . . sixty percent . . . I look forward to positive results from this hypnosis session. (Speak louder and stronger.)

"Four . . . eighty percent, emerging peaceful and happy. (Strongly assert your intention to emerge.)

"FIVE . . . FIVE . . . FIVE . . . One hundred percent now! Wide awake and fully alert!!!"

Overcome Hypochondria

If you feel you are overly concerned with your medical condition, help yourself with this script.

"I am a healthy person.

"I affirm and direct my mind to sustain optimum health and I trust its capability to do so.

"I realize that health challenges may arise from time to time as they do for everyone. Yet I trust and expect my subconscious mind and my body to work together to avert illness and maintain excellent health and wellness.

"I acknowledge that perpetual and unnecessary stress can impair the health of the body. It is known as a 'fight or flight' response to a true and present danger. But when there is no danger, this kind of stress can trigger hormones and other substances in the body that can impair the immune system.

"I want to do everything in my power to allow my immune system to work efficiently and unencumbered. As I decide *to let go of excessive concerns* about my body and its health, I relieve stress so that my body's immune system will function at its best. Since there is no true and present danger, I can feel comfortable freeing my thoughts of constant concerns about health.

"Instead, I choose to identify myself as someone who enjoys the freedom of a *naturally healthy* body and mind.

"I have a strong and amazing immune system that automatically eliminates viral and bacterial infections. My body eliminates toxins and dead cells safely and efficiently. It generates new and vibrantly healthy cells to keep my body functioning beautifully. Millions of processes take place in my body everyday and are handled by my inner mind without any conscious awareness or input. This has been true since the day I was born and continues now and for the rest of my life.

"And because I know that all of these healthy processes are automatic, that means I can focus my attention on other areas of life that truly need my attention. I can choose to focus on my relationships, or my work or my passions. It is wonderful to live my life doing the things that really fulfill me and make me happy.

"I continue to play a conscious part in the health of my body through bathing, proper nutrition and regular exercise. And I continue to get occasional check-ups or diagnostic tests my physician recommends.

"From now on whenever I drink a glass of water, I identify myself—consciously and unconsciously—as a healthy and energetic person. When I feel the pure water on the back of my throat, I am simultaneously purified from unnecessary stress and excessive concerns about health.

"As I go about my life, it feels like my mind is now clear to enjoy all that life and good health can offer."

(The Wake-Up)

"I will emerge gently and easily from hypnosis now by counting from one to five. With each number I emerge twenty percent. When I reach the number five, I will return to everyday awareness.

"One . . . emerging twenty percent, beginning to awaken from hypnosis now. (Speak a little louder and stronger.)

"Two . . . forty percent now, as I become fully aware of my body and environment. (Speak louder and stronger.)

"Three . . . sixty percent . . . I look forward to positive results from this hypnosis session. (Speak louder and stronger.)

"Four . . . eighty percent, emerging peaceful and happy. (Strongly assert your intention to emerge.)

"FIVE . . . FIVE . . . FIVE . . . One hundred percent now! Wide awake and fully alert!!!"

Release Fear of Abandonment

*Eliminate your fear of abandonment
with this script, and add more enjoyment
to all of your relationships.*

"I release the fear of abandonment.

"I am ready to relax and enjoy healthy relationships. In order to do that, I release all fear of being abandoned. Healthy relationships are based on mutual respect and support. Fear has no place in close relationships.

"I see myself in ever increasing measure as an independent and secure person. This self-image allows me to express myself without fear. From now on, I express my opinions, needs and desires so that I can enjoy deep and true relationships.

"Disagreements and adversity in relationships are normal and provide opportunities for development and growth. When problems arise, I learn to relax and be myself at all times. While some problems may result in compromise, I no longer compromise due to any concern about being abandoned by the other person. I make choices from now on that express the respect I have for myself, and balance it with the respect I have for others.

"I may have felt abandoned when I was younger, but it is now time to let go of that memory. Therefore, I imagine sitting on a couch next to my younger self. We watch a video loop of a time when we felt abandoned by someone important to us. Now that I am more mature, the images have no affect on me, but I can see that they are upsetting the younger version of me. As we keep watching, I put my arm around the younger me and say: 'It's just an old video. It cannot hurt you anymore. Everything is okay now.' As I say those comforting words, the younger me calms down. I use the remote control to change the old program to a fun and happier one. It is a scene of me laughing and enjoying the company of others. This makes the younger version of me smile and laugh too.

"I am different now. I am a mature adult. I am wiser, stronger, more independent and secure. I see through the eyes of a mature person who can manage life.

"If I ever again feel insecure or afraid to lose a relationship, I immediately repeat to myself three times, 'I am safe. I am strong. I am okay.' When I do that, the insecure feelings dissolve and I return to a feeling of self-assuredness.

"The new me brings maturity and strength to all of my relationships. I behave in relationships with an ever-growing sense of independence. I know that whatever happens in any relationship, I can handle it. And that is a powerful and positive feeling to have."

(The Wake-Up)

"I will emerge gently and easily from hypnosis now by counting from one to five. With each number I emerge twenty percent. When I reach the number five, I will return to everyday awareness.

"One . . . emerging twenty percent, beginning to awaken from hypnosis now. (Speak a little louder and stronger.)

"Two . . . forty percent now, as I become fully aware of my body and environment. (Speak louder and stronger.)

"Three . . . sixty percent . . . I look forward to positive results from this hypnosis session. (Speak louder and stronger.)

"Four . . . eighty percent, emerging peaceful and happy. (Strongly assert your intention to emerge.)

"FIVE . . . FIVE . . . FIVE . . . One hundred percent now! Wide awake and fully alert!!!"

Override the Fear of Rejection

*Replace the fear of rejection and
prevail in relationships with this script.*

"I override the fear of rejection.

"In the past I may have experienced rejection from an individual or group. After that happened, I made a decision, whether consciously or subconsciously, to fear rejection to avoid feeling hurt in the future. That is what I needed to do at the time to protect myself. But that time has passed. It is time to move on.

"I am ready now to change because the fear of rejection has kept me from being as happy as I deserve to be. Fear of rejection has prompted me to avoid interacting with people and opportunities I need for personal or professional growth.

"With the power of self hypnosis, I override the subconscious pattern of fear and avoidance. I replace it with a feeling of inner strength and calm courage.

"My desire to *feel the pleasure of connection* with others and to seek opportunities that lead to a more fulfilling life far outweighs any concern about rejection.

"Whatever happened in the past is gone now, and can no longer harm me. I have grown *stronger and mature*. I realize that I can handle the natural risks involved in presenting myself to others because I *unconditionally love and accept myself* completely.

"From now on, I anticipate that people are going to like me and enjoy what I bring to relationships. I consider myself a likeable and intelligent person. Everything I express reflects my likability and my natural intelligence.

"Even if someone does not like me for some reason or does not accept what I present to them, I remain strong and self-possessed. My inner core of self-acceptance reminds me I am secure at all times.

"I imagine myself at a pool party. There are friends and strangers in the water enjoying themselves and they invite me to join the fun. Some swim laps while others are on floatation devices. The depth of water is unmarked, but I decide to take a chance to join them in the pool so that I can have fun with them. As I step into the refreshing water, I discover the pool is shallow where I stand. I go a bit farther and the water gets gradually deeper, but I remain safe and in control over how far I go. I have complete freedom to wade, swim or grab a floating device and simply enjoy the company of other people in the pool. I am glad I gave myself permission to take the risk of adventure and have a wonderful time. The risk was worthwhile!

(Pause five seconds.)

"I choose from this day forward to override the fear of rejection so I may live more fully.

(The Wake-Up)

"I will emerge gently and easily from hypnosis now by counting from one to five. With each number I emerge twenty percent. When I reach the number five, I will return to everyday awareness.

"One . . . emerging twenty percent, beginning to awaken from hypnosis now. (Speak a little louder and stronger.)

"Two . . . forty percent now, as I become fully aware of my body and environment. (Speak louder and stronger.)

"Three . . . sixty percent . . . I look forward to positive results from this hypnosis session. (Speak louder and stronger.)

"Four . . . eighty percent, emerging peaceful and happy. (Strongly assert your intention to emerge.)

"FIVE . . . FIVE . . . FIVE . . . One hundred percent now! Wide awake and fully alert!!!"

Okay with Confrontation

With this script, you will boost your confidence and verbally confront others when necessary.

"I feel okay verbally confronting people when necessary.

"In the past, I avoided verbally confronting people. I allowed people to say or do things that negatively influenced me without speaking up for myself. I may have been afraid of my anger. I may have been concerned about how others would react to confrontation.

"I am ready to now release all fears about verbally confronting people.

"Failing to confront others has sometimes made me feel like a coward. Failing to confront others made me feel like I have dishonored myself. Expressing disagreement with others is normal and healthy and helps me to maintain inner harmony and self honor.

"Through the power of self hypnosis I override those fears and confront persons or groups of people whenever I feel justified in doing so. I *stand up for myself* and disallow anyone to disrespect me.

"From this time forward, I act as my own best advocate.

"I acknowledge that verbally confronting a person or even a group of people is sometimes necessary to maintain my self-respect. And sometimes it is necessary to speak up in order to right a wrong that has been done to me.

"I stand up to people when necessary.

"It is good and correct to stand up to other people when they have wronged me. I trust my sense of ethics and morality to know when someone has not treated me right, and it is okay for me to confront them.

"I trust myself to know when it is appropriate to confront a person.

"Many people will respect me for confronting them. I give them opportunity to apologize for any disrespect they have shown me. Some people will not like me when I confront them. Nevertheless, it is more important that I like and respect myself. In fact, I release the need for others to like me.

"I release the desire for everyone to like me.

"Some people may become hostile when I confront them. If people become angry when I confront them, I am okay with their anger. I hold my position and self-respect even when others display anger.

"It is okay for others to get upset when I confront them.

"Standing up for myself does not make me a selfish or hostile person. After I have justifiably confronted someone, I feel very good about myself because I have affirmed my self esteem.

"I am a good person with high self esteem.

"I may think of myself as a peaceful person. I may have held on to the false belief that kind or peaceful people are non-confrontational and that conflict is bad. However, there are many non-violent ways to confront a person. There are many ways to express conflict while maintaining my peaceful disposition.

"Whenever I am faced with a situation in which I think confrontation is required, I draw a slow deep breath and when I release it I repeat silently, 'I'm okay with confrontation.' When I do that, I calmly and immediately speak up and confront the person.

"I imagine waiting in line at a clothing store when a man jumps in line ahead of me. I feel disrespected. I draw a deep breath and quietly think to myself, 'I'm okay with confrontation.' Immediately I say aloud to the man, 'I'm next in line, Sir. You are after me.' The man apologizes and says he had not notice me in line and he then moves behind me.

"Now I picture a situation in which an acquaintance makes a rude and offensive comment. I draw a breath and release it, and repeat to myself, 'I'm okay with confrontation.' In a relaxed manner, I immediately tell that person that I am offended by the comment. The acquaintance is unapologetic and my objection angers them. This makes everyone around us feel awkward. But I'm okay with that. It is okay when others are angry or uncomfortable with me. I do not need everyone to like me or agree with me. And I feel great that I have stood up for myself.

"From now on I am perfectly comfortable when I feel the need to confront someone. As a grown and mature person, it feels wonderful to express disappointment or disapproval when I am upset by a person's words or behavior.

"I'm okay with confrontation from this time forward."

(The Wake-Up)

"I will emerge gently and easily from hypnosis now by counting from one to five. With each number I emerge twenty percent. When I reach the number five, I will return to everyday awareness.

"One . . . emerging twenty percent, beginning to awaken from hypnosis now. (Speak a little louder and stronger.)

"Two . . . forty percent now, as I become fully aware of my body and environment. (Speak louder and stronger.)

"Three . . . sixty percent . . . I look forward to positive results from this hypnosis session. (Speak louder and stronger.)

"Four . . . eighty percent, emerging peaceful and happy. (Strongly assert your intention to emerge.)

"FIVE . . . FIVE . . . FIVE . . . One hundred percent now! Wide awake and fully alert!!!"

Comfortable Expressing Anger

Express your anger in a healthy way
with this script.

"I am comfortable feeling and expressing anger.

"When I was young, I may have been discouraged from expressing anger. Maybe I observed unhappy people who misdirected their anger or were violent or out of control.

"Wherever it came from, I programmed myself to avoid expressing feelings of anger. Perhaps I held my anger inside because I was afraid what others might say or do in response. I might have worried that my anger would get out of control. I may have thought that expressing anger would make me a bad person or cause me to become angry all the time. I might have imagined all sorts of negative consequences to expressing my anger that made me keep it to myself.

"But when I kept silent about angry feelings, the anger may have festered and created inner disharmony of mind and body. I see now that keeping anger bottled up can have many negative consequences.

"I choose to change how I think and feel about expressing anger and how I behave whenever I feel angry. I choose to express my anger in healthy and controlled ways.

"I embrace anger as a healthy and normal human emotion. There are many appropriate reasons for feeling anger. When I express anger in healthy ways, it establishes my personal boundaries. It lets others know when they have infringed upon my psychological or physical boundaries. If I do not reveal when I feel angry, people may not realize when they have wronged me.

"I accept that the expression of angry feelings is an important part of healthy relationships with family, friends, acquaintances and strangers. In addition, I want healthy relationships.

"I dissolve fears about expressing anger. I give myself permission to express anger in non-violent ways, and to let that person or group respond however they choose. It is okay if others get upset or uncomfortable when I express anger.

"I remain in control as I communicate angry feelings and words to others. When I express anger it acts like a steam valve, helping me to safely release feelings so that they do not build up.

"Vocalizing anger is different than being hateful or doing violence. Even the kindest and most peaceful people express anger when necessary. Therefore, when I communicate angry feelings I remain non-violent. I continue to be a good and kind person. I no longer equate the healthy expression of anger with acts of violence or hatred. They are not the same because even good and kind people express anger. So I can feel *comfortable expressing controlled anger* even though I am a good person.

"I imagine that a close friend makes an offensive remark and I feel angry about it. I immediately express my anger saying, 'I feel really angry about your comment.' I permit the emotion to come through my words. My friend looks surprised by my anger, apologizes for offending me, and clarifies the remark. We spend some time discussing the matter and my anger quickly dissipates. We remain close friends, even after I expressed my anger and it feels good to be honest and open with my friend. Our friendship becomes better and stronger because I am willing to be honest when I feel upset.

"As I become more comfortable expressing anger I learn to do so in ways that add to my quality of life and my relationships. Appropriate displays of anger reveal my boundaries and affirm healthy self-esteem.

"So I am comfortable expressing anger when I feel the need."

(The Wake-Up)

"I will emerge gently and easily from hypnosis now by counting from one to five. With each number I emerge twenty percent. When I reach the number five, I will return to everyday awareness.

"One . . . emerging twenty percent, beginning to awaken from hypnosis now. (Speak a little louder and stronger.)

"Two . . . forty percent now, as I become fully aware of my body and environment. (Speak louder and stronger.)

"Three . . . sixty percent . . . I look forward to positive results from this hypnosis session. (Speak louder and stronger.)

"Four . . . eighty percent, emerging peaceful and happy. (Strongly assert your intention to emerge.)

"FIVE . . . FIVE . . . FIVE . . . One hundred percent now! Wide awake and fully alert!!!"

Freedom from Porn Addiction

This script will help you become free of the compulsive desire to view pornographic material.

"I choose to be free of interest in pornography.

"It is time to free myself from any compulsion to view pornography. Through the power of self hypnosis, I reprogram my mind to *break up pornography addiction* so that I can be happier and proud of myself. From this time forward, I channel those desires into activities that provide genuine pleasure and fulfillment.

"Like other addictions, the more time and energy I spent on pornography, the less pleasure it gave me back. I feel embarrassed or ashamed about it, so I have kept it secret. It had become a replacement for excitement, passion and intimacy that are missing from life.

"Sometimes when I have felt bored, I have turned to pornography to distract myself from those feelings. Only, after watching porn, I felt empty and dissatisfied with myself. I felt worse than before. Ultimately, porn does not make me feel good.

"I recognize that porn is a fraud. It is not what it appears to be. It can never offer me true passion or intimacy. The excitement is generated by images on a screen that have nothing to do with me, and in no way enrich my life.

"Addiction to porn is like an abusive relationship. Some people stay in toxic relationships because they do not realize that a good relationship is possible for them.

"Others leave a bad relationship for a while but then return to it, because they do not accept deep down that they deserve a loving and supportive relationship.

"But I know that I can find and *sustain healthy and exciting interests and relationships*. I believe I deserve to be happy and proud of myself in all I do.

"I dedicate myself here and now to seek and find healthy ways to fulfill my authentic need for passion, intimacy and excitement. I invest my time and effort to build interests in real relationships that give me what I truly want and need. There are no substitutes for those healthy and real interests and relationships..

"So I direct my subconscious to *ignore pornographic material* once and for all so that I never feel embarrassed or ashamed again. I *dismiss all interest in pornography*. I divorce myself from pornography, and it feels good to do that.

"I now imagine getting ready to watch some pornography. As pornographic images begin to flash on the screen, I imagine someone I deeply respect or love suddenly standing right beside me watching what I am about to do. And I think about how much their opinion of me matters.

(Take a moment to imagine it.)

"I see the surprise and disappointment on their face. As I do, any interest I had in watching porn completely disappears. As I immediately *turn away from the pornography*, I imagine the person I respect nodding and smiling with approval. They know I am capable of doing better things with my time.

"And I remember that there are other things that I could be doing which interests and excites me. There are passions I would like to explore. There are people I would like to contact and see in person. There is a better life I would like to live. Therefore, pornography no longer has a place in my life.

"Every time I consider returning to porn, I bring the face of that person I love and respect to my mind and I speak their name. When I say their name aloud, I am filled with a sense of deep pride in my growth and I am committed to my well-being. I instantly recall my commitment to fulfilling my passions in healthy and productive ways.

"Now I imagine that I walk along a sidewalk at night in a city. At the end of the block, I can see a luxurious hotel where I have a reservation. However, as I walk toward it there are sordid carnival barkers calling out to lure me into their places to watch pornography. They talk dirty and promise many pleasures if I follow them inside.

"I think of the face of the person I most respect or love, and I speak their name aloud. When I do, the words and promises of the sleazy carnival barkers sound silly, self-serving and hollow. *Any compulsion to watch porn disappears* and is replaced with a fierce determination in me to go directly to the luxurious hotel to enjoy my stay in the city.

"As I bypass every offer to watch porn, I *feel very proud* of myself. And when I reach the luxurious hotel and go inside, the lobby is filled with interesting people who introduce themselves. The concierge offers to arrange activities that match my true passions and interests. There are a lot of exciting things to do and it feels good to have the time and energy to pursue them.

"With every passing day any interest in watching porn fades away until it is a distant memory. I can picture myself a year from now, and that it's hard to remember why I ever had an interest in porn. I have so much more time on my hands to do the things that matter to me now that I am free of porn. I have much better things to do.

"It is good to be free from pornography now and forever."

(The Wake-Up)

"I will emerge gently and easily from hypnosis now by counting from one to five. With each number I emerge twenty percent. When I reach the number five, I will return to everyday awareness.

"One . . . emerging twenty percent, beginning to awaken from hypnosis now. (Speak a little louder and stronger.)

"Two . . . forty percent now, as I become fully aware of my body and environment. (Speak louder and stronger.)

"Three . . . sixty percent . . . I look forward to positive results from this hypnosis session. (Speak louder and stronger.)

"Four . . . eighty percent, emerging peaceful and happy. (Strongly assert your intention to emerge.)

"FIVE . . . FIVE . . . FIVE . . . One hundred percent now! Wide awake and fully alert!!!"

Conquer Compulsive Masturbation

*This script will assist in overcoming
the compulsive desire to masturbate.*

"I choose to be free of the addiction to masturbate.

"It is time to free myself from compulsive masturbation. Through the power of self hypnosis, I reprogram my mind to dissolve the desire to masturbate so I can channel my energies into passions and activities that provide dignified pleasure and healthy fulfillment.

"Obsessive masturbation is like other types of addiction. What was at one time pleasurable, feels burdensome to me now. What was once fun and a normal expression of self-love feels empty and indulgent now. Obsessive masturbation is a waste of time and energy.

"I am ready to overcome the habit of compulsive masturbation.

"When I felt bored, lonely or under-confident, I may have masturbated to distract myself. Only, after masturbating I felt empty and dissatisfied.

"At some point, masturbation became a replacement for stimulation, excitement and intimacy that have been missing from life. Now I am bored with masturbation and realize it can never offer me true passion or intimacy that can only come from growing my relationships with other people. Masturbating can never make up for what may be lacking in my life.

"I acknowledge my responsibility to fill my time with exciting interests and relationships that provide true inner stimulation. I think about how to expand my life and explore new possibilities to live more passionately day to day.

"I dedicate myself here now to seek and find healthy ways to fulfill my authentic need for excitement and intimacy. I invest my time and effort to build interests and relationships that give me what I truly want and need. There are no substitutes for healthy interests and relationships.

"I recall a time when I felt completely bored. Maybe I was kept waiting a long time; maybe other diverting things were not available.

(Take a few moments to
create the emotional state of boredom.)

"I imagine sitting in a dark room watching a video of myself masturbating. I feel *completely unemotional* as I watch myself masturbate. I would rather do just about anything else and get away from this *uninteresting masturbation* video.

"The video goes on for a very long time until I am so bored I cannot endure it anymore. I use the *fast forward* function on the remote control, but I realize this video is an endless loop of masturbating. All I want to do now is *stop the masturbation* images and choose to do something else.

"I repeat to myself, 'I've had enough!' So I press the STOP button on the remote control and the video screen goes blank. I feel embarrassed and the sweat causes me to feel chilly. Suddenly, a door opens behind me and warm sunlight streams in. I get up and walk out of the door and onto a beautiful beach. The color of the sand, sky and water are vivid, the sound and smell of the salty ocean makes me feel alive with pleasure. There are seagulls in the air, dolphins jumping in the water and I see up ahead a group of attractive people playing volleyball. I even consider introducing myself so I *can have fun with them.*

"It feels so good to feel free enough to enjoy every aspect of life. There is so much I want to explore and feel. I do not want to waste a single minute more in the dark watching myself masturbate.

"From now on, I find *masturbation boring.* If I attempt to masturbate again, I say to myself: 'I've had enough!' And when I do, I recognize it is easily within my power to *stop masturbating* and immediately find interesting people and other activities to occupy my time and fulfill my inner need for pleasure and connection.

"I am now free to explore and enjoy life, passion, pleasure and intimacy."

(The Wake-Up)

"I will emerge gently and easily from hypnosis now by counting from one to five. With each number I emerge twenty percent. When I reach the number five, I will return to everyday awareness.

"One . . . emerging twenty percent, beginning to awaken from hypnosis now. (Speak a little louder and stronger.)

"Two . . . forty percent now, as I become fully aware of my body and environment. (Speak louder and stronger.)

"Three . . . sixty percent . . . I look forward to positive results from this hypnosis session. (Speak louder and stronger.)

"Four . . . eighty percent, emerging peaceful and happy. (Strongly assert your intention to emerge.)

"FIVE . . . FIVE . . . FIVE . . . One hundred percent now! Wide awake and fully alert!!!"

Stop Drinking Coffee

*This script is meant to help you
stop drinking coffee for health reasons.*

"I stop drinking coffee.

"Drinking coffee is just a simple habit. And like any habit, it can be changed. Through the power of self hypnosis, I choose to break the coffee-drinking habit quickly and easily so that I am coffee-free.

"As I communicate clearly and directly with my subconscious while I read these words, the change takes full and immediate effect. I am released from the pattern of drinking coffee right now and forever.

"From this day forward the smell of *coffee is disgusting* and the taste of *coffee is putrid*. My senses tell me that *coffee is no longer appealing at all.*

"Many people *cringe when tasting coffee* for the first time. So I imagine tasting plain coffee for the first time. The *coffee tastes bitter* and strange. I spit it out into a rusty bucket of old cigarette butts and look at the ugly swill with disgust.

"I wonder why anyone would ever swallow something that *tastes so foul*. Some people try to cover up the *bad taste of coffee* by adding cream or sugar, but it still tastes terrible.

"As I *stop drinking coffee*, I begin to experience many benefits. I am no longer jittery. My blood pressure returns to normal. I feel calmer and happier. I sleep better. My teeth are whiter and my breath is fresher. My body is able to remain hydrated, and even re-hydrate when I replace the coffee with purified water. Not having coffee allows all my body systems to function much better. It feels good to be coffee-free!

"When I experience the benefits of being completely coffee-free, my desire to *remain coffee-free* doubles up. When I see other people drinking coffee, it does not bother me at all: it only affirms my decision to remain healthy and coffee-free.

"I replace coffee with another heated beverage: tea or water with lemon—as long as it's healthy. I drink it at the times I used to drink coffee. As the better hot liquid fills my stomach, I am satisfied and realize how much I prefer it over coffee. And, every sip of the healthy, coffee-free beverage reminds me how much happier and healthier I feel.

"I imagine eating lunch with a friend in a restaurant. At the end of the meal, my friend orders a cup of coffee while I order a hot, coffee-free beverage. I notice the unappetizing scent of the coffee as it is poured into the cup. As my friend drinks it, I quietly observe coffee stains on her teeth. I am aware that after drinking a few sips, her energy appears erratic because of the high dose of caffeine in the repulsive brew. I feel wonderful to be free of the negative effects of drinking coffee. As I sip from my hot beverage, I think of how my teeth remain unstained by coffee, how my nerves are calm, how I'm in a good, even-tempered mood and how my health is better. It feels good to *say 'No' to coffee.*

"Thanks to the power of self hypnosis, I completely *bypass the withdrawal symptoms* associated with caffeine. I feel just fine.

"When I emerge from this self hypnosis session, I will be delighted to discover that I have lost all interest in coffee. I simply do not want it anymore. Then I will *feel empowered* because I have proven to myself how easy it is to *take control* over my own behaviors and choices.

"I recognize my mind's power to make new choices that lead me to greater health and happiness. I realize how easy it is to let go of coffee, and to make wiser selections. After a month of remaining coffee-free, the idea of drinking coffee will seem ridiculous and like a distant memory.

"I am now and shall remain coffee-free."

(The Wake-Up)

"I will emerge gently and easily from hypnosis now by counting from one to five. With each number I emerge twenty percent. When I reach the number five, I will return to everyday awareness.

"One . . . emerging twenty percent, beginning to awaken from hypnosis now. (Speak a little louder and stronger.)

"Two . . . forty percent now, as I become fully aware of my body and environment. (Speak louder and stronger.)

"Three . . . sixty percent . . . I look forward to positive results from this hypnosis session. (Speak louder and stronger.)

"Four . . . eighty percent, emerging peaceful and happy. (Strongly assert your intention to emerge.)

"FIVE . . . FIVE . . . FIVE . . . One hundred percent now! Wide awake and fully alert!!!"

Eat Less Chocolate

This script will help you eat less chocolate.

"I choose to be free from the habit of eating chocolate.

"The habit of consuming chocolate is much like any other habit. Habits can easily be changed with the help of self hypnosis. With the assistance of self hypnosis I commit and direct my entire mind and body to *eat less chocolate.*

"With every passing week, I choose to *eat less chocolate.* When I *eat less chocolate,* I find I actually *want less of it.* Within one month from when I first read this script, any compulsive desire to eat chocolate will be completely gone. Self-control and better health replaces it.

"I picture myself sitting in front of a large video screen. On the screen is a picture of a vegetable which I have sometimes chosen to eat but do not really care for.

(Think of a vegetable you eat which
is less appealing.)

"I feel completely unemotional about this food and it really doesn't matter whether I ever eat it again. It is of no interest to me. Next, the video shows the uninteresting vegetable multiplying so there is a great abundance of it on the screen. Then, the video shows many different ways the vegetable may be prepared. Nevertheless, I continue to find it uninteresting no matter how it looks, no matter how it is prepared.

"The video now changes and shows a bar of chocolate. I feel just as uninterested in the chocolate bar as I do about the vegetable. The image of chocolate has little appeal to me. The screen then shows many different types of chocolate candies and desserts, but I feel emotionally detached from the idea of chocolate no matter what form of it is presented on the screen. The video goes on for a long time and I realize it's taking up so much of my time. So I press the STOP button on the remote to turn off the images of chocolate. I decide, instead, to go do things that are more interesting now, to build my confidence and to make me feel good about my life.

"In ever increasing measure, I feel emotionally detached from the image of chocolate on the screen of my inner mind. I am more and more interested in doing things that stimulate my mind and body and fill me with pleasure.

"I commit both consciously and subconsciously to eat *fifty percent less chocolate* next week than I eat this week. The week after next, I commit to consuming another fifty percent *less chocolate*. So each week I decide to eat fifty percent less chocolate than the week before.

"Within a month's time I will discover that I eat a very small amount of chocolate and no longer eat it every day. The habit of wanting or needing to eat chocolate completely dissolves.

"I imagine it is one month from today. Each week I successfully ate less and less chocolate. Whenever I look at a piece of chocolate I feel indifferent about it. I have complete freedom to decide whether to eat it or let the chocolate go. I feel marvelous about my new sense of self control.

"With this wonderful freedom of choice, I decide to pursue activities and relationships that make me feel really good inside and out. And as I do, I find the habit of eating chocolate has been replaced with activities that truly add to the quality and joy of life."

(The Wake-Up)

"I will emerge gently and easily from hypnosis now by counting from one to five. With each number I emerge twenty percent. When I reach the number five, I will return to everyday awareness.

"One . . . emerging twenty percent, beginning to awaken from hypnosis now. (Speak a little louder and stronger.)

"Two . . . forty percent now, as I become fully aware of my body and environment. (Speak louder and stronger.)

"Three . . . sixty percent . . . I look forward to positive results from this hypnosis session. (Speak louder and stronger.)

"Four . . . eighty percent, emerging peaceful and happy. (Strongly assert your intention to emerge.)

"FIVE . . . FIVE . . . FIVE . . . One hundred percent now! Wide awake and fully alert!!!"

Love Cleaning House

This script will help you to want to clean your home regularly.

"I enjoy cleaning my home.

"From now on I take delight in each and every activity associated with cleaning and straightening my living space. Through the power of self hypnosis I reframe my thinking to recognize the value and meaning that household chores provide.

"I love to clean my home because it provides exercise I need. Whether it's vacuuming, doing the laundry or putting away the dishes, each activity requires the use and movement of various muscles, which adds tone and strength to my body. The more housework I perform, the stronger and fitter I get.

"Housework burns many calories and helps me keep my weight in check. So when it is time to perform a given chore, I do it with vigor and enthusiasm because my body can use the exercise to make me fitter and healthier.

"I enjoy housework because it has a deep meaning. I see my home as a metaphor. It represents me. And I now recognize cleaning my home is a symbolic way to improve my thoughts, feelings and behavior.

"I enjoy cleaning and tidying rooms in my home because I find that the more I put things in their proper place the clearer and more logical my thinking becomes each day.

"Anytime I want to improve the clarity of my thinking, I straighten and tidy my home. This provides my inner mind a suggestion to de-clutter my thoughts and put the day's concerns into proper order and perspective.

"I love cleaning house because it fills me with pride and a sense of accomplishment. Whenever I finish cleaning or straightening up, I will take a moment to feel the satisfaction about what I have just done. I notice I not only *feel good about the task,* I also *feel good about myself.* Cleaning and maintaining my living space reaffirms my self-respect which positively impacts how I think and feel each day.

"Whenever I clean or tidy any part of my house, I say to myself, 'I maintain my life efficiently with great self respect.' As I do that, I discover improvements in the health and quality of my body, my thoughts and my behavior.

"Now that I understand that housework is a valuable use of my time, I look forward to it as never before. Immediately following this self hypnosis session, I will have *the inclination to clean and tidy* some part of my *home.* I will do it gladly. And I will think about the many rewards I receive as I go about the housework tasks.

"I love doing housework, because it makes me happier, healthier and satisfied."

(The Wake-Up)

"I will emerge gently and easily from hypnosis now by counting from one to five. With each number I emerge twenty percent. When I reach the number five, I will return to everyday awareness.

"One . . . emerging twenty percent, beginning to awaken from hypnosis now. (Speak a little louder and stronger.)

"Two . . . forty percent now, as I become fully aware of my body and environment. (Speak louder and stronger.)

"Three . . . sixty percent . . . I look forward to positive results from this hypnosis session. (Speak louder and stronger.)

"Four . . . eighty percent, emerging peaceful and happy. (Strongly assert your intention to emerge.)

"FIVE . . . FIVE . . . FIVE . . . One hundred percent now! Wide awake and fully alert!!!"

Break Shopping Addiction

This script is to help overcome the addiction of shopping for unnecessary merchandise.

"I stop shopping for things I do not need.

"With the help of self hypnosis, I reprogram my subconscious mind so I may let go of any desire to shop excessively. I overcome shopping addiction.

"People sometimes do excessive things without knowing why. But there is always a secret reason. Some people eat too much because they don't feel fulfilled. They eat excessively as a way to compensate for that. Some people smoke in excess to feel calm and secure, because they haven't learned healthy methods, like self hypnosis, to quickly relax and center themselves.

"The reason some people shop too much is to feel a sense of control and satisfaction that is otherwise missing. And now that I recognize the reason I have been shopping so much, I can *let go of shopping addiction* and get my needs met in healthier ways.

"I seek out new and wise ways to feel in control and fulfill my needs and desires that leave out needing to purchase unnecessary merchandise. From this moment forward, I find healthy ways to feel control and satisfaction in my life.

"From now on, whenever I see items for sale, or whenever I stand at a cash register, I carefully consider my potential purchase. I ask myself, 'Do I really need this at this time?' If the answer is yes, then I purchase the item and complete the transaction. If the answer is no, a surge of confidence and willpower rises within me, and then I easily stop myself from purchasing the item.

"It is easy and enjoyable for me to say 'No' to unwise or unnecessary purchases. Whenever I say 'No' to buying things, I feel in control, resolute and powerful. So I no longer need or want to purchase things in order to feel a sense of control. My new way to experience power and control feels much better than the old way I felt after buying things I don't need.

"I also find wonderful ways to experience satisfaction. I bring to mind activities that make me feel excited and passionate which have nothing to do with shopping or merchandise. As I immerse myself in those activities, I discover what true satisfaction feels like. And if necessary, I *explore new interests* so I may awaken new passions and experience satisfaction through them.

"In a few moments when I emerge from self hypnosis, any compulsive interest in buying things will have completely evaporated. In its place will be a new and healthy desire to feel powerful when I say 'No' to purchasing unnecessary merchandise, and a glorious anticipation of finding satisfaction through my interests and passions.

"From this moment on I have healthy purchasing habits."

(The Wake-Up)

"I will emerge gently and easily from hypnosis now by counting from one to five. With each number I emerge twenty percent. When I reach the number five, I will return to everyday awareness.

"One . . . emerging twenty percent, beginning to awaken from hypnosis now. (Speak a little louder and stronger.)

"Two . . . forty percent now, as I become fully aware of my body and environment. (Speak louder and stronger.)

"Three . . . sixty percent . . . I look forward to positive results from this hypnosis session. (Speak louder and stronger.)

"Four . . . eighty percent, emerging peaceful and happy. (Strongly assert your intention to emerge.)

"FIVE . . . FIVE . . . FIVE . . . One hundred percent now! Wide awake and fully alert!!!"

Stutter Anxiety Relief

This script will help reduce
stressful feelings about stuttering.

"I become anxiety-free about stuttering.

"Many experts say there is a relationship between stuttering and stress. I also may have noticed that when I feel anxious, I tend to stutter more. On the other hand, when *I feel relaxed* I may notice how *words flow more easily.*

"Through the power of self hypnosis I *let go* of stress and eliminate nervous tension about stuttering in any and all situations. When I do I discover from now on I *stutter less* when I speak.

"As I read these words aloud in a relaxed state of self hypnosis … in a place where I feel completely safe and calm … I may stutter very little or not at all. There may be long periods of time when I am *completely stutter-free.*

"Stress and anxiety are part of the body's fight or flight response. When people are in danger, stress can be a helpful response. When *there is no threat,* there is no reason to trigger the fight or flight response.

"In the past, I may have triggered the fight or flight mechanism accidentally because I was afraid how others might react to me. My body responded to my fear, which interfered with the part of my brain associated with vocal communication. Through self hypnosis I now inform my body that there is *nothing to fear* when I speak. I can *relax and speak freely.* I am safe and all is well.

"As I *choose to relax* when I *talk* to people, my nervous system and the speech center in my brain function harmoniously. And when they do, I stutter less or *forget to stutter* altogether.

"From now on, right before I speak to a person, I can take a nice, slow deep breath and as I exhale I pretend I am breathing out any and all anxiety. And as I speak, I feel completely safe and comfortable taking my time and allowing the words to come out.

"I imagine now that I am standing in front of someone very important who has asked me a question. Before I answer, I take a deep breath and as I exhale I imagine releasing all worries about what I say or how I say it. The important person patiently waits for my answer and I feel completely safe and at ease. I realize I have the freedom to take my time and let my words formulate. As I answer the question I hear the words flow smoothly, easily and effortlessly from my mouth. It is great to feel safe and relaxed and to just let myself talk.

"With every day that passes I feel more at ease right before I talk to people. I gain freedom from stress and anxiety about stuttering and as I do, I learn I am able to *communicate more smoothly* in conversation.

"As my body remains in a peaceful state, the part of my mind that deals with my speech center functions harmoniously. Because my body and mind feel secure, I find that I forget to worry about stuttering, and let words flow without a second thought.

"It feels good to relax about how I speak, and to concentrate on important things. From now on, I look forward to just being myself. I am free to relax and express myself in whatever way comes naturally. I am safe, relaxed and all is well."

(The Wake-Up)

"I will emerge gently and easily from hypnosis now by counting from one to five. With each number I emerge twenty

percent. When I reach the number five, I will return to everyday awareness.

"One . . . emerging twenty percent, beginning to awaken from hypnosis now. (Speak a little louder and stronger.)

"Two . . . forty percent now, as I become fully aware of my body and environment. (Speak louder and stronger.)

"Three . . . sixty percent . . . I look forward to positive results from this hypnosis session. (Speak louder and stronger.)

"Four . . . eighty percent, emerging peaceful and happy. (Strongly assert your intention to emerge.)

"FIVE . . . FIVE . . . FIVE . . . One hundred percent now! Wide awake and fully alert!!!"

Overcome Blushing

*Reduce or eliminate blushing caused by
your emotions with this script.*

"I control myself from blushing.

"Blushing sometimes happens when a person feels angry or embarrassed in social situations. It is an display of emotional intelligence and self awareness. It's a natural process controlled by the sympathetic nervous system. And the sympathetic nervous system is controlled by the subconscious mind. The subconscious may be controlled through hypnotic suggestion. So it makes perfect sense to me that I can *control blushing* through self hypnosis!

"I choose to relieve all concern about blushing in social settings when I accept that it's just a natural indication of my emotional intelligence. By dissolving that fear, and deciding that occasional blushing is okay, I can now relax and be myself in public. And the less I care about blushing, the less I blush. So I can feel unconcerned about my natural reactions in social situations . . . and enjoy myself . . . and enjoy my conversations. If something happens and I think I might blush, I think to myself 'So what?' and move on in the conversation. As I think 'So what?' any sign of momentary blushing fades within a few seconds.

"I picture myself at a party with friends and acquaintances. Someone makes a harmless joke at my expense that embarrasses me. Right then, I decide to let my reactions naturally happen. I simply relax, whether I am blushing or show no sign of it, and I think to myself 'So what?' and let go of any concern about it whatsoever. When I do that, I discover any feelings of embarrassment pass very quickly, and I feel very comfortable as the conversation turns to something else.

"I also have the option to exercise control over my body and mind when I feel embarrassed or angry in public. Those emotions speed the heartbeat and the breathing and trigger tiny blood vessels in the face to become wider. When they widen, more blood flows through them, which gives skin a red, rosy appearance. So blushing is a response to heated emotions. I can learn to cool my emotions to *reduce the blushing easily.*

"As I gain mastery of my emotions in social situations, I can reduce or *eliminate blushing altogether.* I reduce the intensity of any emotion by taking charge of my breathing. Whenever I feel embarrassed, angry or feel any other uncomfortable emotion, I calm and regulate my breathing. As I silently think to myself *'frosty blue,'* I will slow down my breathing and imagine that the air is a *frosty blue* color and a calmness and self-control will quickly return to my mind and my body.

"I now imagine myself in a restaurant with my friends and some strangers. Then someone says something embarrassing. This time, I choose to control my reactions. I think to myself *'frosty blue.'* While others talk, I silently and secretly slow down my breathing. I quietly imagine as I breathe in and out that the air is a cool blue color. And after about three slow breaths, the feeling of embarrassment neutralizes and my face immediately retains its normal color.

"No one around me knows that I used self hypnosis to stop myself from blushing. And that gives me a surge of confidence and self-mastery so I can feel even more comfortable in social settings.

"As I grow more and *more comfortable and confident* with myself in social situations, I realize that concerns about blushing get smaller and smaller . . . a thing of the distant past . . . until the issue just doesn't matter to me . . . and I *forget about blushing* altogether.

"I realize the less I care about it, the less I blush . . . until there comes a time . . . when I feel comfortable in my own skin . . . when blushing is not even in my thoughts.

"And now I can *just relax*, stay cool and enjoy myself . . . in any social situation."

(The Wake-Up)

"I will emerge gently and easily from hypnosis now by counting from one to five. With each number I emerge twenty percent. When I reach the number five, I will return to everyday awareness.

"One . . . emerging twenty percent, beginning to awaken from hypnosis now. (Speak a little louder and stronger.)

"Two . . . forty percent now, as I become fully aware of my body and environment. (Speak louder and stronger.)

"Three . . . sixty percent . . . I look forward to positive results from this hypnosis session. (Speak louder and stronger.)

"Four . . . eighty percent, emerging peaceful and happy. (Strongly assert your intention to emerge.)

"FIVE . . . FIVE . . . FIVE . . . One hundred percent now! Wide awake and fully alert!!!"

Never Be Late Again

Don't be tardy for your scheduled appointments ever again with this script.

"I choose to never be late again for appointment and commitments.

"I banish all the reasons I have for running late, because they are just rationalizations. Through the power of self hypnosis, I dissolve any inclination to be late for scheduled commitments. With determination and the power of my subconscious mind, I establish a new and permanent pattern of being early for work or personal obligations so I am never late again.

"Everyone is responsible for managing their time. I do not like to be kept waiting and I recognize that others do not appreciate waiting for me. I take full responsibility for the management of my schedule and I do everything in my power to manage it efficiently.

"In the past, I may have planned things up to the last minute, allowing no leeway for natural or unexpected delays. From now on, I set *realistic timeframes* for each of my activities. I accurately put aside ample time for me to bathe, dress, complete my errands and include travel time so I can *arrive slightly early* for my appointments.

"I manage my schedule beautifully and efficiently.

"Punctuality shows that people respect each other's time. Because I want to express how much I honor other people, I *decide to arrive early* for any meeting, event or get-together I attend. Arriving early guarantees I am there on time and demonstrates my respect for others.

"I imagine I have a lunch engagement planned with important friends at noon. As I wake up in the morning, I look forward to arriving at the restaurant ten minutes before noon. I plan and prioritize the tasks and chores I can undertake in the morning before my lunch date, and how long it will take me to travel to the restaurant. As I carefully evaluate the timeframe, I realize that in order to arrive at 11:50 some chores must be postponed. So I make the choice to save some tasks for a later time so I can *honor my commitment* to my friends.

"I feel relaxed as I go about my morning tasks because I have plenty of time to do them all. Instead of feeling rushed and overwhelmed, I feel calm and happy. I arrive at the restaurant at 11:47, and am delighted to be the first to arrive. The server leads me to a table where I comfortably wait for my friends. I relax with a glass of my favorite beverage.

"As my friends arrive, they smile and comment on how wonderful it is to see me on time. We enjoy each other's company. And I feel fantastic that I am here on time to experience every minute with them.

"I enjoy life so much more as I plan to *arrive early* for all of my commitments and appointments. Not only will I see the difference in improved relationships with friends, family and colleagues, but I will feel an inner calm because I am orderly and prepared which gives me much more confidence and self-respect. Those are excellent reasons for creating this new pattern of thought and action to *arrive early* to meet all of my obligations in a timely manner.

"I now imagine it is one year from now and that arriving early for commitments has become a longtime habit for me. People no longer make jokes about me being late, because I *am never late*. I no longer feel embarrassed that I am rushed. I have completely changed my relationship with time, and it has improved my relationships and the quality of my life.

"It feels good knowing I will *never be late* again."

(The Wake-Up)

"I will emerge gently and easily from hypnosis now by counting from one to five. With each number I emerge twenty percent. When I reach the number five, I will return to everyday awareness.

"One . . . emerging twenty percent, beginning to awaken from hypnosis now. (Speak a little louder and stronger.)

"Two . . . forty percent now, as I become fully aware of my body and environment. (Speak louder and stronger.)

"Three . . . sixty percent . . . I look forward to positive results from this hypnosis session. (Speak louder and stronger.)

"Four . . . eighty percent, emerging peaceful and happy. (Strongly assert your intention to emerge.)

"FIVE . . . FIVE . . . FIVE . . . One hundred percent now! Wide awake and fully alert!!!"

Tennis Focus

*When you play competitive tennis, become
more confident and focused on your game and
match play with this script..*

"I improve my tennis game.

"I now program my mind though the power of self hypnosis to advance and enhance my tennis game in every way. By doing so, I reach new levels of mastery with my tennis strokes and experience more satisfaction from my matches.

"Every shot in tennis practice and match play is registered by my mind. I trust my mind to automatically calculate and *adjust my accuracy* in ever greater measure. The more I practice and play, the more precise my mind's calculations and anticipation.

"I feel at ease whenever I first step onto the court, whether to practice or play a match. I have a keen and intuitive sense of the entire court. My feet are light and active. My body remains loose and agile. Light and active … loose and agile.

"I *watch the ball* and wait for it to come into my strike zone before hitting it. I keep my eyes on the ball, and when I stroke it with my racket, I exhale to generate more power.

"When preparing to use my forehand or backhand, I am on the balls of my feet. When my opponent hits the ball, I turn and move toward the ball. My mind rapidly calculates how long it will take me to get to the ball so that I can arrive at just the right time.

"I take lots of little steps to get into the final position to strike the ball. I keep my arm loose to create racquet speed.

My eyes remain on the ball as I strike it and exhale. I feel the stroke and follow through to complete the shot.

"After hitting the ball, I immediately get back into position to prepare for the coming rally. I wait until the end of a point to admire my shots.

"On my serve, I first draw and release a slow, deep breath to relax and keep my body loose. I bounce the ball, and shift my weight to the back leg as I lift and toss the ball into the air. My head remains still as I intensely watch the ball before I strike it.

"After I hit my serve, I immediately get into position to prepare for the opponent's return.

"I play my matches one point at a time. I reset my focus between every point by saying to myself silently, 'Next point.' When I do that, it signals my mind and body to release the stress of the previous point and to concentrate on the new point.

"Whenever I win a point, I allow myself to enjoy the moment and admire my shot. Then I reset my concentration by saying, 'Next point.'

"Whenever I lose a point or make an error, I stay calm and relaxed and say to myself: 'Next point.' As I do, I forgive the mistake and look forward to the opportunity the next point provides me.

"After this session, I will experience greater happiness and satisfaction as I notice excellent improvements in my tennis game. By learning and practicing tennis skills and trusting my mind and body to work together with harmony and precision, there is no limit to how far I can progress as a tennis player."

(The Wake-Up)

"I will emerge gently and easily from hypnosis now by counting from one to five. With each number I emerge twenty

percent. When I reach the number five, I will return to everyday awareness.

"One . . . emerging twenty percent, beginning to awaken from hypnosis now. (Speak a little louder and stronger.)

"Two . . . forty percent now, as I become fully aware of my body and environment. (Speak louder and stronger.)

"Three . . . sixty percent . . . I look forward to positive results from this hypnosis session. (Speak louder and stronger.)

"Four . . . eighty percent, emerging peaceful and happy. (Strongly assert your intention to emerge.)

"FIVE . . . FIVE . . . FIVE . . . One hundred percent now! Wide awake and fully alert!!!"

Sports Excellence

To practice for competitive sports, this script boosts your focus and confidence.

"I have excellent *focus and optimal* performance as I play my sport.

"I now program my mind though the power of self hypnosis to *maximize mental concentration* and *boost coordination* and athletic ability whenever I play the sport of my choice. By doing so, I achieve *higher* levels of performance and experience greater satisfaction from my sport.

"Maximize concentration. Boost Coordination.

"I practice my sport with enthusiasm because there is no substitute for practice. The greatest athletes in all sports practice vigorously and with precision to achieve and maintain excellence, so I *embrace practice*. Through practice, I gain strength, dexterity and skill to play my sport with ever increasing mastery. The more I practice, the more excellently I perform. I look forward to practicing my sport so that when I compete I have access to all of the power and experience of a sports champion.

"Practice brings mastery.

"Every physical movement and mental state I've ever experienced while practicing or playing my sport is recorded in my mind. I trust my mind to *automatically calculate and adjust* my accuracy and power to optimize my athletic performance. Thus, the more I practice and play, the more precise my mind's calculations and anticipation.

"Calculate. Adjust. Optimize.

"I take a moment to think about a time when I played a sport and performed exceptionally well.

(Take a few seconds and vividly recall
a moment of excellence.)

"During that time, my mind and body communicated and worked together harmoniously. My sense of power and coordination were *spot on*. It felt great being in the moment and observing myself performing so beautifully. Everything flowed with precision and all of my reactions and responses were perfectly executed. It was great fun to *see myself in the zone.*

"*Spot on. Flow with precision. In the zone.*

"My subconscious remembers perfectly the mental and physical states needed to *perform with excellence*. In addition, I can call upon my subconscious to initiate those states from now on so I can *perform with excellence* whenever I play my sport.

"Before or during any game, match or athletic competition, I say to myself, 'Spot on. Spot on. Spot on.' When I do that, my subconscious automatically and immediately heightens my athletic ability and power. My mind and body at that time call upon all of my training and experience to reenter the zone of excellence and *perform at peak levels.*

"*Spot on. Re-enter the zone. Perform at your peak.*

"Whenever I use the post-hypnotic cue: 'Spot on. Spot on. Spot on,' I can stop over thinking and simply trust the lightning speed of the communication between my mind and body that put me in that zone of peak performance. I know I am at my best and it feels great!

"After I emerge from this self hypnosis session, there will remain a *sense of power* in my ability with sports and with life in general. It is as though I have discovered a great secret to access the excellence in my mind, body and performance. I will excel at whatever sport I do and draw upon my inner and outer resources to achieve peak performance whenever I desire.

"From this day forward, I experience greater excellence and that feels great!"

(The Wake-Up)

"I will emerge gently and easily from hypnosis now by counting from one to five. With each number I emerge twenty percent. When I reach the number five, I will return to everyday awareness.

"One . . . emerging twenty percent, beginning to awaken from hypnosis now. (Speak a little louder and stronger.)

"Two . . . forty percent now, as I become fully aware of my body and environment. (Speak louder and stronger.)

"Three . . . sixty percent . . . I look forward to positive results from this hypnosis session. (Speak louder and stronger.)

"Four . . . eighty percent, emerging peaceful and happy. (Strongly assert your intention to emerge.)

"FIVE . . . FIVE . . . FIVE . . . One hundred percent now! Wide awake and fully alert!!!"

Be More Psychic and Intuitive

Increase your psychic sensitivity and your intuition with this script.

"I am more psychic and intuitive with every passing day.

"My subconscious mind already possesses amazing intuitive abilities. In the past, many of these abilities remained dormant or unrecognized. I now use the power of self hypnosis to awaken these intuitive abilities to bring their benefits to my everyday life.

"I safely awaken more of my natural intuitive ability.

"My awareness of psychic impressions increases as my connection with my subconscious develops. Because self hypnosis relaxes my body and mind and places me in closer connection to my subconscious, performing self hypnosis on a regular basis automatically strengthens my intuitive awareness.

"In ever increasing measure, I experience hunches that turn out to be accurate. I know things before they happen. I am able to tell what people are thinking and feeling. Happy and lucky coincidences occur for me on a regular basis.

"Every day I think about myself as intuitive. I look to apply my gifts in practical ways, both for personal benefit and for the good of others.

"Just as people have many skills or talents they draw upon to assist their lives, I have intuitive gifts and use them to make my life better and more productive.

"I expect my psychic powers to manifest ever stronger and with greater frequency from now on. As I welcome and expect psychic experiences to appear in my life, my subconscious fulfills that expectation and makes it a reality.

"I pay attention for a few moments now on the space between and just above my eyebrows known as the Third Eye. I imagine there is a beautiful indigo colored jewel there that glows brightly and makes my mind like a two-way radio. I can send and receive psychic knowledge and impressions to produce greater harmony and abundance in my life. I send psychic messages anytime I concentrate on people or circumstances that are important to me. My mind filters the impressions I receive and supplies my conscious mind with only important content.

"Whenever I relax and concentrate on the indigo jewel between my eyebrows and think the words, 'Psychic power now,' my psychic power increases momentarily and I become especially tuned to psychic waves of intuition and thought.

"I use my reasoning mind to carefully consider the knowledge and intuitions I receive through my psychic senses. Whenever possible I verify what I receive before acting on the information. My intellect works together with my psychic senses to make sensible choices.

"I use my psychic abilities responsibly. I trust my moral and ethical compass to apply my psychic abilities wisely without taking unfair advantage of others.

"Every day brings new insights and opportunities to manifest these amazing natural mind powers. I look forward to exercising and developing these abilities so that they become stronger. Every day, I become more psychic and intuitive."

(The Wake-Up)

"I will emerge gently and easily from hypnosis now by counting from one to five. With each number I emerge twenty

percent. When I reach the number five, I will return to everyday awareness.

"One . . . emerging twenty percent, beginning to awaken from hypnosis now. (Speak a little louder and stronger.)

"Two . . . forty percent now, as I become fully aware of my body and environment. (Speak louder and stronger.)

"Three . . . sixty percent . . . I look forward to positive results from this hypnosis session. (Speak louder and stronger.)

"Four . . . eighty percent, emerging peaceful and happy. (Strongly assert your intention to emerge.)

"FIVE . . . FIVE . . . FIVE . . . One hundred percent now! Wide awake and fully alert!!!"

QUESTIONS

In this chapter, I will answer frequently asked questions about the as-you-read self hypnosis method:

Q: If I did not feel hypnotized during the inductions, does it mean it did not work for me?

A: No. Many people feel nothing in particular when they are hypnotized, but this does not indicate failure. When you read an induction you may not feel anything unusual. You will know the method is effective when positive changes appear within hours or days afterwards.

Q: Do I have to read the scripts aloud to get results?

A: Many deaf readers of my books have told me they have gotten terrific results by reading the scripts silently. However, for hearing readers I recommend using the "read aloud" technique because hearing the sound of your own voice is a powerful part of the method. If you choose to read the scripts silently, be sure to read them extremely slowly. You will diminish your results if you race through them.

Q: Can I record the scripts and play them back instead of reading them aloud?

A: You may certainly record the scripts and play them back. I have already produced many professional-quality mps if you enjoy listening to hypnosis audios. Go to my webpage to see what is available: www.forbesrobbinsblair.com/mish-mp3s-main.html.

However, there are powerful hypnotic components in the read-aloud method that recorded audios cannot reproduce, so only use the audios as a supplement.

Q: Can I use multiple scripts in a day for more than one goal at a time?

A: Yes, you can work on multiple goals, but make sure to separate your sessions by several hours. For instance, you might work with the "Drop the Last Ten Pounds" script in the morn-ing and the "Social Anxiety Relief" script in the even-ing. However, I do not recommend using more than two scripts in a single day.

Q: How many times should I perform sessions for each goal?

A: Repeat your sessions once a day for consecutive days until you achieve the intended results. Some goals will only require one, two or three applications, while others may re-quire up to 21 daily sessions or even more. Many people have reported faster results by performing their sessions twice a day, separated by several hours.

Q: Can I switch induction scripts for a goal?

A: Yes. You may choose any of the four inductions for any given self hypnosis session.

Q: What is the best time of day to use the self hypnosis as-you-read method?

A: Choose a time for your sessions when you will not be disturbed. Some people have reported excellent results when they use it before bedtime; other users prefer mornings shortly after waking. Whatever works for you is truly your best time.

Q: Why are the goal scripts relatively short?

A: It is my experience that long scripts do not produce better results. This has been verified for me over the last 15 years with hundreds of clients, students and email contacts. These self hypnosis scripts are kept purposefully short so a session can be completed in 20 minutes or less. Also, it is far more effective to repeat shorter scripts daily than to perform longer scripts sporadically.

Q: Are the scripts a substitute for medical or psychological treatment?

A: Absolutely not! The scripts in this book are offered with the understanding that the author and publisher are not engaged in rendering legal, medical, psychological, or any other kind of professional advice or service. If that is required, the services of a competent professional person should be sought.

Q: Can I write my own suggestion scripts for topics not covered?

A: Yes. Instructions about how to write an effective script are available in my first book, *Instant Self Hypnosis: How to Hypnotize Yourself with Your Eyes Open*. With its guidance, you can learn how to hypnotize yourself while writing a script at the same time!

ADVANCED

There are several ways to make the self hypnosis as-you-read method more powerful. You may use these *advanced* but simple techniques to deepen the hypnotic state in order to make your mind even more receptive to the therapeutic suggestions.

The basics of this method are usually sufficient to achieve results. However, if you are the kind of person who wants to optimize the potential of the method, then one or more of these advanced techniques may be incorporated. Keep in mind these advanced techniques will lengthen your sessions.

Advanced Technique #1:
The Five Second Pause

The easiest way to make the method more powerful is to read the scripts *very slowly*. However, many people ignore that or forget to apply it. Pay special attention whenever you see the dots (…) and take a *five-second pause* before continuing to read the script.

Also… when you use any induction, be sure to read the words slowly and follow any instructions between the parentheses. By read-ing slowly, you will hypnotize yourself deeper and the suggestions will be well-received by your subconscious mind.

Advanced Technique #2:
Pause Before the Wake Up

After you finish reading the suggestions for your goal, pause 30 seconds before starting the Wake Up. During this 30-second pause just sit quietly. You do not need to read or think about anything in particular. Just relax. Then, after 30 seconds read the Wake Up as usual to end the session. This technique allows the mind and body to breathe, so to speak, and it assists in the absorption of the therapeutic suggestions.

Do not underestimate this simple yet advanced technique!

Advanced Technique #3:
Read More Than One Induction

One of the most powerful ways to take yourself deeper into self-hypnosis is to read aloud more than one induction before commencing with the goal script of your choice.

Begin by reading any one of the induction scripts. When you reach the end, immediately turn to any of the other inductions and read it aloud as well. When you reach the end of the second induction, move on to your bookmarked goal script and read it as you would normally.

Advanced Technique #4:
Read Entire Session Twice in a Row

To experience a truly profound state of self hypnosis and become ultra receptive to the therapeutic suggestions, perform the entire session twice in a row. That is, begin by reading an induction script, and then read the goal suggestion script and the Wake Up. Then…immediately repeat the entire session from beginning to end!

This technique involves a phenomenon known to hypnotists as *fractionation*. Essentially, it means that by emerging yourself from hypnosis and then going back into hypnosis immediately to reach a deeper level. Just make sure after the second reading to finish with the Wake Up.

SUPPORT

It's hard to believe ten years have passed I wrote my first book, *Instant Self Hypnosis: How to Hypnotize Yourself with Your Eyes Open.*

While I believed in my eyes-open hypnosis discovery from the start, I had no idea my scripts would help so many people all over the world—or that I would write three more books about self hypnosis.

Thank you for allowing me to share my discoveries and passion with you. There is no greater thrill for me.

You can achieve your dreams and goals with these life-changing self hypnosis scripts. However, you have to work with the scripts for a few consecutive days for each goal. Setting aside the same time each day works best.

Make a commitment to yourself. You are just a few sessions away from changing your life. You can do it!

If you have any questions or suggestions, please contact me at webmaster@forbesrobbinsblair.com.

AUTHOR

Forbes Robbins Blair is a professional hypnosis therapist, author, entrepreneur and originator of the Hypnosis As-You-Read with Your Eyes Open Method. He believes that changing your behavior should not be difficult. Self hypnosis makes it the easy and fast.

Typically, self hypnosis requires script memorizing and can take up to an hour of your valuable time. With his hypnosis as-you-read method, your sessions take just 15-20 minutes with immense results!

Forbes writes his books to encourage people to change habit patterns with hypnosis. His explanations are straight-forward. His scripts are full of positive imagery. His mission is to empower people to change negative habits into positive ones.

Self Hypnosis As You Read: 42 Life-Changing Scripts is his fourth book. He has written three other books on hypnosis including the bestselling *Instant Self Hypnosis: How to Hypnotize Yourself with Your Eyes Open*. He has created eBooks and multimedia programs about the Law of Attraction and self-growth. He began teaching his innovative self hypnosis methods in 1997 and has since appeared on national radio and television or his expertise.

Mr. Blair lives in Montgomery Village, Maryland. Visit his site: www.forbesrobbinsblair.com

Editor & Designer

Robert Morrison is a graduate with a Master's Degree in Counseling Psychology from Stanford University. He has worked for several years in the fields of writing, website design and editing. Since 2001, he has made major contributions to Forbes Robbins Blair's trade paperbacks *Instant Self Hypnosis, Self Hypnosis Revolution* and *More Instant Self Hypnosis.*

He also co-wrote with Mr. Blair the Law of Attraction/ Hypnosis eBook and audio program called Genie Within: Your Wish Is Granted.

You can find the webpage that describes Genie Within here: www.forbesrobbinsblair.com/geniewithin.html

Robert is also narrator for the More Instant Self Hypnosis Mp3 Audio Products on Forbes' website: www.forbesrobbinsblair.com/mish-mp3s-main.html

Mr. Morrison did the book interior layout and editing/ proofing for this book. You can email him about his services here: robubc@yahoo.com

RESOURCES

More Instant Self Hypnosis:
Hypnotize Yourself as You Read

Written in 2011, and updated in 2013, this book offers 48
eyes-open self hypnosis scripts. Script topics include: "Low
Carb Diet," "Attract a Mate," "Job Interview Confidence,"
"Go to the Gym," "Reduce Smoking Easily," "Emotion
Control," and dozens more. It includes a valuable chapter
about how self hypnosis affects the subconscious mind's
ability to help achieve your goals. Also featured is the Master
Induction 2.0 and five powerful bonuses including: self
hypnosis session deepeners and how to use this method to
hypnotize other people. This book is the sequel to *Instant Self
Hypnosis.*

More Instant Self Hypnosis Mp3 Audios

Based on scripts from the book, these powerful hypnotic mp3
audios are convenient, private and talk directly to you. They
feature special theta-wave technology that assures success.
Most are less than 20 minutes long and very effective. They
include an induction, post-hypnotic suggestions and wake up.
Here's the site: www.forbesrobbinsblair.com/mish-mp3s-
main.html

Instant Self Hypnosis:
How to Hypnotize Yourself with Your Eyes Open

The original bestseller teaches you an easy-to-use self
hypnosis method to enter a hypnotic state to improve your life
as you read aloud with no willpower needed! It includes
wonderful suggestion scripts like *"Have Great Sex," "Stop
Procrastinating,"" Overcome Fear of Public Speaking," "Feel*

More Energetic" and 31 more. My first book is available in trade paperback, digital eBook and at most book retailers.

Self Hypnosis Revolution:
The Amazingly Simple Way to
Use Self Hypnosis to Change Your Life

My second book started as a book of affirmations. I changed that focus to show you *how to reprogram your mind for success during your everyday routines using autosuggestion and imagery*. Break bad habits, heal emotional wounds, increase physical and mental well-being, make more money and improve relationships and spirituality. It takes just minutes to learn this technique that can lead to a lifetime of empower-ment for you. Bring a little desire and dedication and this book will do the rest (with an assist from your subconscious mind). Available in trade paperback at major booksellers.

The Genie Within:
Your Wish is Granted

This is a law of attraction/self hypnosis eBook and audio mp3 program (in basic and deluxe versions)—that reveals how to acquire and use your own "magic" lamp to manifest your fondest desires while you make the most of the Law of Attraction. The lamp and the genie are powerful symbols for your fiery intention and the seemingly magical power of your subconscious mind. You can attract love, manifest money or just about anything else you want with this powerful original method. Available as an instant downloadable eBook and mp3 package on Forbes' Genie Within webpage: www.forbesrobbinsblair.com/geniewithin.html